Portsmo
An A

Peter Harris, the highest goal
scorer in the club's history, attacks
the Bolton goal.

Dean Hayes

S.B. Publications

To Pompey fans everywhere

First published in 1997 by S. B. Publications,
c/o 19 Grove Road, Seaford, East Sussex BN25 1TP

ISBN 1 85770 148 8

Designed and typeset by CGB, Lewes
Printed by MFP Design and Print
Longford Trading Estate, Thomas Street,
Stretford, Manchester M32 0JT

F A Cup Final 1939

Jimmy Guthrie receives the FA Cup from King George VI after Pompey's 1939 triumph.

ACKNOWLEDGEMENTS

The author wishes to thank the following for their invaluable assistance in producing this book:

Portsmouth Football Club, the staff of the Central Reference Library, Portsmouth, and particular thanks to the club's Number One fan – Mick Cooper.

PICTURE CREDITS

Illustrations were kindly supplied by *The News,* the *Lancashire Evening Post* and Peter Stafford. A number are from the author's own collection.

ABOUT THE AUTHOR

Dean Hayes is an experienced freelance sports writer specialising in football and cricket.

He was educated at Hayward Grammar School, Bolton and West Midlands College of Physical Education. He was a primary school head teacher until taking up writing full-time two years ago.

Having played football in the Lancashire Amateur League, he now concentrates solely on playing the Summer sport. This former cricket professional, now playing as an amateur, recently took his 2,000th wicket in League cricket.

Dean is married, with two children, this is his twentieth football book to be published and his thirty-ninth overall.

Portsmouth Football Club
A–Z

A

ABANDONED MATCHES

A MATCH which is called off by the referee while it is in progress because conditions do not permit it to be completed. Generally speaking, far fewer matches are now abandoned, because if there is some doubt about the ability to play the full game, the match is more likely to be postponed.

In the first round of the 1919–20 FA Cup competition, Southern League Pompey were drawn away to First Division Bradford City. Despite going a goal down, they completely outplayed their hosts on a waterlogged pitch and two goals in a minute by Stringfellow and Turner gave them a half-time lead. In the second half, the conditions deteriorated and after the home side had scored a disputed equalising goal, the referee, who was unable to find the centre spot for Portsmouth to resume the match, abandoned it. The game was replayed a week later with the First Division club winning 2–0.

During the 1941–42 London War League game against Aldershot, the referee had to abandon the game after Andy Black headed the crossbar, and the post snapped at the base, an immediate repair not being possible.

ABERDARE ATHLETIC

They spent six seasons in the Third Division (South) from 1921 to 1929 when they failed to gain re-election. The two clubs first met on 27 August 1921, the opening day of the season. The match was Aberdare's first Football League game and ended goalless. The return fixture at Fratton Park a week later also ended all-square at 2–2. The following season saw Pompey complete the 'double' over their Welsh opponents and in the first

5

game of the 1923–24 season, Billy Haines scored a hat-trick in a 4–0 win for Pompey. The last time the clubs met was on 17 March 1924 with the same result as when they first met – a goalless draw.

AGGREGATE SCORE

Portsmouth's highest aggregate score in any competition came in the Football League Cup second round match against Blackpool. Pompey won the first leg at Fratton Park 4–0 and the return at Bloomfield Road 2–0.

AIZLEWOOD, STEVE

Born in Newport, South Wales, Steve Aizlewood made his League debut for his home town club at the age of sixteen and became the youngest player in Newport County's history to make 100 League appearances. After scoring eighteen goals in 1987 League games, he was sold to Swindon Town in March 1976 for £13,000 as the County Ground club sought a replacement for Frank Burrows.

Aizlewood joined Pompey in the summer of 1979 as a replacement for Steve Foster in one of the first transfers to require the new Football League fee arbitration system. Swindon eventually received £90,000 which was less than they had hoped for.

He made his debut for the Fratton Park club in the opening game of the 1979–80 season, a 3–0 win at Hartlepool United going on to help the club win promotion to the Third Division. In 1982–83 Aizlewood won a Third Division championship medal but at the end of the following season, after playing in 201 League and Cup games for Pompey, he was allowed to leave and joined Waterlooville.

ALDERSHOT

In March 1992, the liquidator who had been called in to supervise the winding up of the 'Shots' confirmed to the Football League that no offers had been received for the then Fourth Division club.

The two clubs met on four occasions with Pompey winning both games at the Recreation Ground, yet failing to win either of the Fratton Park encounters. The clubs first met in 1978–79 when **Pompey** won 2–0 away from home and drew 1–1 at home in the final game of the season.

The following season, Pompey won promotion from the Fourth Division and though they won 2–1 at the Recreation Ground, they went down 3–1 at home on New Years Day.

ALLEN, JIMMY

Signed from his home town club, Poole, Jimmy Allen made his debut for Portsmouth on 28 January 1931 in a 2–1 defeat away to Birmingham City. He was ever-present in 1932–33 and this was also the season when he scored his only goal for the club in a 2–0 win over Wolverhampton Wanderers.

Allen won a runners-up medal in the FA Cup Final of 1934 when Pompey were beaten 2–1 by Manchester City. He was an important member of the Pompey side and it was an injury to him that turned the game City's way. The Fratton Park club were leading 1–0 when he had to leave the field. Manchester City snatched victory with two goals from Fred Tilson. The rumours that Allen had died from his injuries happily proved untrue.

With Pompey, Allen made two full appearances for England and two for the Football League. Just seven weeks after the FA Cup Final and after he had made 145 League and Cup appearances for Pompey, he joined Aston Villa for £10,775 – a British record fee for a non-forward. The transfer was an on-off affair and centred around a dispute over a benefit. Most clubs paid £650 but Pompey were only offering the international centre-half £400. He eventually moved on but only after a last minute intervention from the Villa chairman.

With their fee for Allen, Portsmouth built their North Stand and to this day it is still referred to by many as the 'Jimmy Allen' Stand.

Allen captained the Villa side which won the Second Division title in 1937–38 and played in 147 League games for the Midlands club. Like most players of his time, his career was spoiled by the Second World War and though he 'guested' for Pompey during the hostilities, he was forced to retire through injury in 1944.

AMATEUR INTERNATIONAL PLAYERS

Four Portsmouth players have won amateur international honours, the first being Lionel Louch who appeared for England at centre-forward in the 6–1 win over Sweden in Gothenburg on 8 September 1908. He was followed by Ernest Williams in 1909. Albert Egerton Knight played in thirty-one amateur internationals for England, winning an Olympic gold medal in 1912 when the United Kingdom beat Denmark 4–2 in the final in Stockholm. Pompey's last amateur international was Patrick Neil who made three appearances for England at outside-left in 1955.

ANDERTON, DARREN

After showing early promise, the Southampton-born winger made his Pompey debut in a goalless draw at home to Wolverhampton Wanderers in November 1990. Towards the end of that season, he was challenging strongly for a first team place and in 1991–92 established himself in the side.

He came into the national spotlight during the club's long FA Cup run, scoring both goals in the fourth round defeat of Leyton Orient and another brace in the remarkable 4–2 fifth round victory over Middlesbrough at Ayresome Park. In the semi-finals, he scored a breakaway goal against Liverpool which looked like taking Pompey to their first ever FA Cup Final for fifty-three years until the Reds' last minute equaliser.

Soon after the end of that season, he joined Tottenham Hotspur for £1.75 million. Despite his career at White Hart Lane being dogged by injuries, he has appeared in more than 150 first team games and represented England in all five matches of Euro '96.

ANGLO-ITALIAN CUP

Portsmouth first entered the competition in 1992–93 when they beat Charlton Athletic (Away 3–1) and drew with Millwall (Home 1–1) in their preliminary round matches to qualify for the next stage. Their results against the Italian sides were:

Cesena (Home. Won 2–0) Bari (Away. Lost 0–3)
Lucchese (Home. Won 2–1) Ascoli (Away. Won 2–1)

yet Pompey did not qualify for the semi-finals.

In 1993–94, the club won both their preliminary round matches, beating Bristol City (Home 3–1) and Oxford United (Away 2–0).The results of their matches against the Italian clubs were:

Padova (Away Drew 0–0) Pescara (Away Lost 1–2)
Cosenza (Home Won 3–0) Fiorentina (Home Lost 2–3)

and so yet again failed to qualify for the semi-final stages.

APPEARANCES

Jimmy Dickinson holds the record for the greatest number of appearances in a Portsmouth shirt, with a total of 834 games to his credit between 1946 and 1965. In all Dickinson played 764 League games, forty-nine FA Cup games, fifteen League Cup games and five other games including an appearance in the FA Charity Shield. He also made thirty-one appearances during wartime football.

The club's top ten players in terms of appearances made are:

	League	FA Cup	F.Lg Cup	Others	Total
Jimmy Dickinson	764	49	15	6	834
Alan Knight	640	39	49	21	749
Peter Harris	479	37	0	4	520
Johnny Gordon	443	29	12	5	489
Harry Harris	380	24	22	2	428
Jack Weddle	368	28	0	0	396
John Milkins	344	27	18	0	389
Alex Wilson	350	18	9	4	381
Albert McCann	338	22	19	0	379
Phil Gunter	321	25	13	6	365

ASPINALL, WARREN

The Wigan-born utility player began his career as an apprentice with his home town club and made his League debut in a 1–1 draw against Leyton Orient on 2 March 1985. He was able to play in midfield or attack and went on to score twenty-two goals in fifty-one League games for the Latics before he joined Everton for £150,000 in February 1986.

Finding his first team opportunities at Goodison Park limited, he moved to Aston Villa for £300,000 a year later. He had scored fourteen goals in forty-four League games for the Villans when in August 1988 he signed for Portsmouth for a then club record fee of £315,000.

The former England Youth international played in 159 first team games for the Fratton Park club scoring twenty-eight goals, including eleven in his first season when he was second to Mick Quinn in the goalscoring charts. After loan spells with Bournemouth and Swansea City, he joined the Cherries on a permanent basis on the final day of 1993 before signing for Carlisle United, where he scored the club's first ever live TV goal in the 4–2 defeat of Wycombe Wanderers.

ATTENDANCES: AVERAGE

Portsmouth's average home League attendances over the last ten years have been as follows:

1986–87	13,390	1991–92	11,789
1987–88	15,923	1992–93	13,706
1988–89	10,201	1993–94	11,692
1989–90	8,959	1994–95	8,269
1990–91	9,689	1995–96	9,407

ATTENDANCES: HIGHEST

The highest ever attendance at Fratton Park is 51,385 for the sixth round FA Cup game between Portsmouth and Derby County on 26 February 1949. Pompey won 2–1 with both goals scored by Ike Clarke.

ATTENDANCES: LOWEST

The lowest ever attendance at Fratton Park for a first team fixture was on 5 December 1989 when a crowd of 2,499 turned up to see Pompey entertain Wimbledon in a Zenith Data Systems Cup second round match. The Dons won 1–0 but lost at Ipswich Town in the next round.

AWAY MATCHES

Portsmouth's best away wins have come in the Southern League, Division Two, when they beat Chesham 7–0 on 30 March 1912 and in the London Combination when Queen's Park Rangers were defeated 7–1 on 2 December 1916.

Pompey's best away win in the Football League came at Newcastle United on 15 November 1930 when two goals apiece from Jack Smith, Jack Weddle and Jimmy Easson plus one from Fred Cook gave the club a 7–4 victory.

Portsmouth's worst defeat away from home is 10–0, a scoreline that occurred at Tottenham Hotspur in a London Combination match on 31 March 1917 and at Leicester City on 20 October 1928 in what was a First Division game. Pompey were also involved in two other high scoring away games, losing both matches 7–4, the first at Chelsea in 1957–58 and the second at Charlton Athletic in 1960–61.

AWAY SEASONS

The club's highest number of away wins came in 1961–62 when they won twelve of their twenty-three matches in winning the Third Division championship. The highest number of goals Pompey have scored away from home is thirty-nine in that same championship-winning season.

AWFORD, ANDY

An influential member of the Pompey Youth side which reached the semi-finals of the 1990 FA Youth Cup, he made his League debut in a 2–0 defeat at Crystal Palace on 15 April 1989, when aged just sixteen years and 275 days old.

Awford, who is capable of playing as a sweeper or as an old fashioned centre-half, became a regular England Under-21 international, producing some outstanding form during England's magnificent triumph in the 1993 Toulon Under-21 tournament.

Despite having suffered from a number of injuries in recent seasons, including a broken leg, he continues to give good service to the club and on 6 April 1996 in his 200th game for them, scored his first goal in Pompey colours in a 2–1 win at Watford.

B

BALL, ALAN

Alan Ball's transfer broke the British record twice. When he moved from Blackpool to Everton in 1966, he cost the Goodison club £110,000 and when he joined Arsenal in 1971, he cost a new record £220,000 fee. He was capped seventy-two times by England and he played a major role in England's World Cup win of 1966. He later played for Southampton, Blackpool and Bristol Rovers before retiring in 1984 with 743 League appearances under his belt.

In May of that year, Ball was appointed Portsmouth's manager and in 1986–87 he steered them into the First Division. Unfortunately Pompey were relegated straight back the following season. With the Fratton Park club again struggling in the Second Division, Ball was sacked.

He later managed Stoke City, Exeter City and Southampton before taking charge of Manchester City.

BARTON, TONY

After representing England at schoolboy and youth level, Tony Barton signed professional forms for Fulham. He made forty-nine League appearances for the Craven Cottage club before joining Nottingham Forest in December 1959. He never really settled at the City ground and two years later he joined Pompey for a fee of £5,000.

He made his debut in a 2–2 draw against Swindon Town on 16 December 1961 and went on to appear in fifty-eight consecutive League and Cup games before injury brought his run of appearances to an end. He played the last of his 144 first team games for Pompey in which he scored thirty-seven goals on 27 August 1966 before retiring to join the club's coaching staff.

He made his first real impact in management with Aston Villa, guiding the club to a European Cup Final victory four months after being appointed as successor to Ron Saunders. After being sacked, he managed Northampton Town but was forced to leave a year later after a heart attack. He was later assistant manager to Chris Nichol at Southampton and caretaker manager of Portsmouth after the dismissal of Alan Ball.

BASEBALL

On 6 June 1918, Fratton Park housed its first ever baseball game. A bemused crowd of Pompey fans watched the United States beat Canada 4–3 with the British Red Cross being the beneficiaries.

BEEDIE, WILLIAM

Left-winger William Beedie was born in Montrose and played his early football for local club Blantyre Celtic before moving to Fratton Park in 1920. He was a tricky player with a devastating turn of speed and played his first game for the club in the 3–0 win over Swansea Town on 28 August 1920,

Pompey's first game in the Football League. He played in exactly half of the club's fixtures in that 1920–21 season but the following campaign he was present in all matches as they finished third in Division Three.

Beedie was a superb crosser of the ball and he made many a goal for Haines, Mackie and Watson but at the end of the 1925–26 season, after scoring twenty nine goals in 216 games, he left Fratton Park to sign for Oldham Athletic.

BERESFORD, JOHN

After beginning his career as an apprentice with Manchester City and winning Youth international honours, he was still unable to force his way into the City first team. In the summer of 1986, he was snapped up on a free transfer by Barnsley and a few weeks later made his League debut against Crystal Palace.

He had appeared in 100 League and Cup games for the Oakwell club when in March 1989 he was transferred to Portsmouth for £300,000 – a fee Barnsley manager Allan Clarke claimed he could not refuse because it was far higher than his own valuation of the player. His Pompey debut was as a substitute in a 1–0 defeat at Leeds United.

Beresford was generally first choice left-back although he did lose his place for a short time to both Ray Daniel and Gary Stevens. He created quite a stir during the club's 1991–92 FA Cup run to the semi-final and in July 1992, after playing in 132 first team games for Pompey, he joined Newcastle United for £650,000.

He had an outstanding first season on Tyneside and was called up to the England squad for the World Cup match in Turkey. One of the best left-backs in the country, his surging runs out of defence have made him a great favourite with the Magpie's supporters.

BEST START

Portsmouth were unbeaten for the first thirteen games of the 1948–49 League Championship winning season, when they won nine and drew four of their matches. Their first defeat came on 23 October 1948 when they lost 3–0 at Wolverhampton Wanderers.

BILEY, ALAN

After scoring seventy-four goals in 165 League appearances for his first club, Cambridge United, the charismatic Biley joined Derby County. After scoring nineteen goals in forty-seven League games for the Rams, Biley was on the move again, this time to First Division Everton. He was only given sixteen full League appearances in which he scored three goals at Goodison before Pompey manager Bobby Campbell invested £125,000 in the ebullient Biley.

He scored his first goal for the club within twenty minutes of his debut in a 4–1 win over Sheffield United. His first hat-trick for Portsmouth came in a 4–1 victory over Lincoln City, who were top of the League at the time. At the end of the season in which Pompey won the Third Division championship, Biley had scored twenty-three goals plus another three in Cup competitions. He had become the first Portsmouth striker since Ron Saunders to break the twenty-goal barrier.

The Leighton Buzzard-born player rapidly achieved folk-hero status and revelled in the adoration of the Portsmouth fans. Unfortunately new Pompey manager Alan Ball did not share the fans universal approval for Biley and in March 1985, he was sold to Brighton and Hove Albion. He had scored fifty-one goals in 105 League appearances for the Fratton Park club, a ratio that does not do justice to the striker. It certainly does not mirror the quality of his goals or his rapport with the fans.

BLAKE, NOEL

Jamaican-born Noel Blake started his football in the West Midlands playing for Sutton Coldfield Town and was on Walsall's books as an amateur before joining up with Aston Villa. He gained further experience at Shrewsbury Town on loan before joining neighbours and rivals Birmingham City for £55,000 and this is where he first started to make his name.

A £150,000 transfer to Portsmouth followed and he made his debut in a 1–0 win over Middlesbrough on the opening day of the 1984–85 season. One of only two ever-presents that season, he did not miss a game in 1985–86 either as Pompey finished fourth in the Second Division on each occasion. Blake played in ninety-six consecutive League games from his debut and went on to appear in 173 first team games, scoring fourteen goals.

At the end of the 1987–88 season, he was given a free transfer by Pompey and joined Leeds United. The circumstances of the free were later to be discussed as, in effect, Alan Ball when he was manager of Stoke City paid £160,000 to Leeds for a man who less than two years before he had 'given away' but he insisted that the Pompey Chairman had dictated the fee.

At Stoke, Blake appeared in seventy five League games before playing for Bradford City and Dundee. He later joined Exeter City as assistant manager.

BLYTH, BOB

Signed from Preston North End by Frank Brettell in 1899, the Ayrshire-born half-back made 175 appearances for the Fratton Park club before replacing Brettell as player-manager in July 1901.

In his first season in charge, he guided the club to the Southern League championship after signing England internationals Arthur Chadwick from Southampton and Steve Smith from Aston Villa. In an attempt to retain the title, he brought in Fred Wheldon, another England international and brought Sandy Brown back from Spurs, but it was not enough and the club finished third.

There then followed a summer of controversy after the signing of three players from Liverpool – Raybould, Goldie and Glover. An FA Commission was set up to investigate the dealings and Blyth was suspended until January 1903 without wages and the club fined £100.

After a comparative lack of success and before the start of the 1904–05 season, Blyth relinquished his post as manager. An uncle of the great Bill Shankly, he later served Pompey as a director and chairman of the club.

BONNEY, RICHARD

Richard Bonney became a director of Portsmouth FC in 1900 but relinquished his position on the Board to take charge of playing matters following the departure of Bob Blyth. He worked hard to strengthen his playing staff, signing goalkeeper Fred Cook from West Bromwich Albion and John 'Sailor' Hunter from Liverpool, but the season was a disappointment.

He spent another busy close season and signed Irish international Harry Buckle and Southampton defender Jack Warner. The club then proceeded to finish the 1906–07 season as runners-up in the Southern League and beat Manchester United after a replay in the FA Cup.

However, after the club finished the 1907–08 season in ninth place, manager Bonney resigned, later to be replaced by Bob Brown.

BRADFORD PARK AVENUE

Park Avenue enjoyed forty-seven seasons in the Football League before failing to hold on to their place in 1969–70 after three consecutive seasons at the bottom of the League. They started their career in the Second Division in 1908–09 and in 1914 joined their Bradford neighbours, City in the First Division. Relegated in 1920–21 they suffered the embarrassment of dropping straight into the Third Division (South) the following season.

They were promoted in 1928 and were not relegated again until 1950–51. Founder members of the Fourth Division in 1958 they won promotion just before their eventual demise.

The two clubs met in 1961–62 when Pompey, who won promotion that season as champions of the Third Division, won 4–2 at home but lost 2–1 away.

BRETTELL, FRANK

One of the most respected men in football, Frank Brettell had started as secretary-player with the St Domingo club in Liverpool and was one of the founder members of Everton. In his playing days, he turned out in nearly every position for the Goodison club. He later transferred to Liverpool and played a major part in the development of that club before becoming secretary of Bolton Wanderers. In 1897, he came south to manage Tottenham Hotspur, introducing the club to the Southern League and persuading a number of northern stars to join them.

He left Spurs when offered a substantial rise to manage Pompey. Building his team from scratch, the club finished their first season in the

Southern League as runners-up to the White Hart Lane club. However, after another season in which the club finished third in the Southern League, Brettell moved to Plymouth Argyle in an attempt to start another club off towards ultimate Football League membership.

BROTHERS

There have been a number of sets of brothers that have played for Pompey but without doubt, the most famous were Jack and William Smith.
They were born in Whitburn and both arrived at Fratton Park from South Shields – Jack in December 1927 and William in June 1928.
Inside-right Jack Smith was an England international, scoring four goals in his three appearances for his country. For Portsmouth, he scored sixty-nine goals in 289 League and Cup appearances. Full-back William Smith played in 325 first team games, scoring just two goals. The brothers played together in 209 League and Cup games during their careers at Fratton Park.

BROWN, BOB

Bob Brown was appointed secretary-manager of Southern League Portsmouth in June 1911. The club had just been relegated and faced financial ruin if they could not regain their First Division status quickly, for the Second Division of the Southern League meant much more travelling and smaller attendances. Fortunately for the club and its fans, Pompey won the Second Division championship and were promoted.
To help boost the club's flagging fortunes, Brown signed a number of Scottish players and in 1919–20 took the club to the Southern League First Division championship. However, in April 1920, he left Fratton Park after a difference over future policy with club chairman George Lewin-Oliver.
After a brief spell as manager of Gillingham, he rejoined Sheffield Wednesday, for whom he had earlier scouted. Success took some time to come to Wednesday but in 1928–29 and 1929–30 he led the club to the League Championship.

BROWN, SANDY

Alexander 'Sandy' Brown was born in Glenbuck, a small village which produced other Scottish international players. He played with St Bernards and Preston North End before moving to Portsmouth for their first season in 1899–1900.

Although Brown was one of a contingent of Scottish players helping to launch Pompey, one newspaper reporter felt compelled to inform his public that Brown was known as 'Sandy' as a common adaptation of Alexander and that it had nothing to do with his hair colouring.

In that first season, Brown scored thirty-four of Pompey's 110 goals, including hat-tricks against Cowes (FA Cup 10–0) and Queen's Park Rangers (Southern League 4–2). His talents were quickly spotted by Spurs and his transfer secured. Brown's impact was immediate, for it was his goals that were responsible for Spurs' first ever FA Cup victory at the end of his initial season. He scored both Spurs' goals in the 1901 Final and then added the deciding strike in the Final replay to give him fifteen goals and a goal in every round.

Having played for the Anglo-Scots in an international trial, he was selected for the full Scotland side against England in 1902, but the ill-fated match was subsequently declared void due to the Ibrox disaster.

In May 1902 he was allowed to return to Fratton Park and though he only spent one season with the club, he proved his effectiveness by scoring 31 goals. He then joined Middlesbrough where he at last won a Scottish cap.

BUICK, ALBERT

Albert Thorogood Buick played his early football with his home town club Arbroath before joining Hearts. He spent five years at Tynecastle and in 1902–03 represented the Scottish League in their annual match against the English League.

The giant centre-half signed for Portsmouth in May 1903 and made his first team debut in a 2–1 defeat at home to Southampton in the opening Western League fixture of the following season.

He was a mainstay of the Pompey side over the next eight seasonsplaying in 310 first team games for the Fratton Park club, 227 of which were in the Southern League. This total was equalled by Jack Warner and only bettered by William Smith.

BURROWS, FRANK

As a player, Frank Burrows was a tough, uncompromising defender and helped Swindon Town to promotion from the Third Division and to a shock League Cup Final victory over Arsenal.

After 297 League appearances for the Robins, he became their assistant manager but in 1978 joined Portsmouth as coach. He succeeded Jimmy Dickinson as Pompey's manager and led the club to promotion to the Third Division in his first season in charge.

After they had consolidated their status in the Third Division, he left to take charge at Cardiff City, but in 1989, he returned to Fratton Park to work as John Gregory's assistant. When Gregory moved on, Burrows took charge for a second time. However, the results were poor and in March 1991, he resigned his position as manager, later taking over at Swansea.

BUTLER, ERNIE

Ernie Butler was playing at left-back in the Bath and District League when

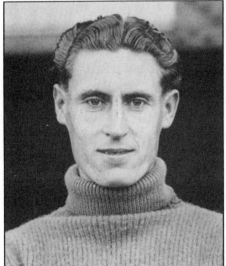

his sides' goalkeeper suffered an injury. Being the tallest player in the team, he was chosen to take his place.

He never looked back, for after Bath City had taken him on, he joined Portsmouth in May 1938. Though he played in the club's last wartime game, he had to wait until October 1946 before making his Football League debut in a 4–1 win over Sunderland.

He was the club's only ever-present in their consecutive League championship successes of 1948–49 and 1949–50.

The arrival of Norman Uprichard from Swindon put a question mark over Butler's future but then in December 1952, he broke a wrist while playing for the reserves and his distinguished career was at an end.

The bone did not knit properly, and at the end of the campaign his wrist was still in plaster. He decided to retire, even though he was offered terms by the club for the following season. Butler had appeared in 240 League and Cup games, keeping eighty-one clean sheets.

BUTTERS, GUY

This England Youth international first impressed with the Hillingdon district team and Middlesex County before joining Tottenham Hotspur as an apprentice in July 1986. Two years later he turned professional and made his first team debut in a League Cup tie at Blackburn Rovers. Finding first team opportunities limited at White Hart Lane, he moved to Portsmouth in September 1990 for £375,000.

Once in the side, he proved himself a solid and dependable central defender and in 1992–93 played a major role in the club's late bid for promotion in which they won twelve of their last fourteen games.

In 1995–96 he began the season as captain and led by example as the club went through a very difficult period, eventually finishing just one place above the relegation zone. Last season he made just ten first team appearances before being allowed to leave the club.

C

CAMPBELL, BOBBY

Bobby Campbell had three spells at Fratton Park – as a player, coach and manager. He built a reputation as a coach with Portsmouth, Queen's Park Rangers and Arsenal before entering management with Fulham. He made almost £1 million in profit on transfer fees during his stay at Craven Cottage but this weakened the side and after they were relegated in 1979–80, he was sacked.

He became Pompey's manager in March 1982 and in his first full season in charge took the club to the Third Division championship. His reward was a three year contract to go with his award of Third Division Manager of the Season. Surprisingly, after a season of consolidation in the Second Division, Campbell was sacked with just one match of the 1983–84 season to play.

CAPACITY

The total capacity of Fratton Park in 1997 was 26,452 with seating available for 6,652 and covered standing for 2,700.

CAPS

The most capped player in the club's history is Jimmy Dickinson who won forty eight caps for England.

CAPS (ENGLAND)

The first Portsmouth player to be capped by England was Danny Cunliffe when he played against Northern Ireland on 17 March 1900. The most capped player is Jimmy Dickinson with forty-eight caps.

CAPS (NORTHERN IRELAND)

The first Portsmouth player to be capped by Northern Ireland was D R A Hanna who played against Wales in 1899. The most capped players are Colin Clarke and Norman Uprichard with thirteen caps.

CAPS (SCOTLAND)

The first Portsmouth player to be capped by Scotland was Jimmy Easson who played against Austria on 16 May 1931. The most capped player is Jimmy Scoular with nine caps.

CAPS (WALES)

The first Portsmouth player to be capped by Wales was Freddie Cook who played against Scotland on 29 October 1927. The most capped player is Kit Symons with eighteen caps.

CAPTAINS

Among the many players who have captained the club are Jimmy Guthrie who led Pompey to their one and only FA Cup triumph in 1939 and Reg Flewin who captained the club when they won the League Championship in 1948–49 and 1949–50.

CENTENARY

Founded in 1898, Portsmouth Football Club celebrate their centenary next year, in 1998.

CENTURIES

There are eight instances of individual players who have scored 100 or more League goals for Portsmouth. Peter Harris is the greatest goalscorer with 193 strikes in his Pompey career (1946–1960). Other centurions are Jack Weddle 170; Ron Saunders 140; Duggie Reid 129; Billy Haines 119; Ray Hiron 110; Johnny Gordon 105 and Jimmy Easson 102.

Only two players have made more than 100 consecutive League appearances following their debut and they are Jock Gilfillan with 170 and Norman Piper with 101. Other players to have made 100-plus consecutive League appearances at any time during their career are: Jimmy Dickinson (186); Alan Knight (158); Alex Mackie (136); Cliff Parker (126); Jerry Mackie (123); Ron Saunders (109) Jimmy Dickinson again (109); George Clifford (101); Jimmy Easson (101) and Ernie Butler (101).

CHAMBERLAIN, MARK

After winning England schoolboy honours, winger Mark Chamberlain made his League debut for Port Vale in a 2–2 draw with Scunthorpe United in August 1978. He had appeared in 110 first team games for Vale when, in the summer of 1982, he joined neighbours and rivals Stoke City for £150,000.

At the Victoria Ground, he won the first of eight England caps, scoring in the 9–0 win over Luxembourg at Wembley. He went on to play in 125 games for the Potters before moving to Sheffield Wednesday for £300,000. He never really settled at Hillsborough, playing more than half his games

as substitute and in August 1988 joined Portsmouth for £200,000.

A superb crosser of the ball, he made his debut in a 4–0 home win over Leeds United, scoring one of the goals. He was hampered by injuries at Fratton Park and his best season was 1992–93 when Pompey finished third in Division One, losing out to West Ham United in the bid for automatic promotion.

Chamberlain, pictured left, played in 188 League and Cup games for Portsmouth before joining Brighton on a free transfer and later playing out his career with Exeter City.

CHAMPIONSHIPS

Portsmouth have won the League Championship on two occasions. The first of these was in 1948–49, the club's Golden Jubilee year. After drawing their opening game of the season 2–2 at Preston North End, they then won six consecutive games to go top of the table, scoring fifteen goals and only conceding one. In fact, Pompey did not lose their first match until 23 October, winning nine and drawing four of their first thirteen fixtures. One of these victories was by virtue of a Len Phillips goal, as Newcastle lost 1–0 in front of what was then a record crowd of 46,327.

Pompey clinched the title at Burnden Park, the then home of Bolton Wanderers. Goals from Peter Harris and Ike Clarke gave Portsmouth their first ever win at the home of the Trotters. The championship trophy was presented to the club a week later when Huddersfield Town were the visitors to Fratton Park.

Portsmouth retained the League Championship the following season, although their early results were mixed. The club lost three of its first six matches before beating Everton 7–0 with Duggie Reid grabbing a hat-trick.

By the end of April, the Championship could have gone to one of four clubs – Pompey, Manchester United, Sunderland or Wolverhampton Wanderers. Pompey's tough-tackling Scot, Jimmy Scoular, was given a two-match suspension by the FA after being sent off at Derby County in March, but much to the club's disgust they were the last two matches of the season.

Portsmouth lost the first of these 2–0 at Highbury and so the title hinged on the last game of the season. Pompey had to beat Aston Villa, but if they dropped a point and Wolves beat already relegated Birmingham City, then the Molineux club would be League champions by one point.

Bill Thompson who was deputising for Ike Clarke scored inside a minute and Pompey went on to win 5–1. Wolves thrashed Birmingham 6–1. Both clubs finished on fifty-three points but Pompey lifted the title on goal average.

CHARITY SHIELD

Pompey's only appearance in the FA Charity Shield saw them draw 1–1 with Wolverhampton Wanderers at Highbury on 19 October 1949 with Duggie Reid scoring the goal. Both clubs retained the shield for six months.

CLARKE, COLIN

Portsmouth was the eighth club of this much-travelled striker. He started his career as an apprentice with Ipswich Town, but failing to make the first team at Portman Road, he joined Peterborough United on a free transfer. After playing in eighty-two League games for the London Road club he joined Tranmere Rovers after a loan spell at Gillingham. At Prenton Park, he scored twenty-two goals in forty-five appearances before moving to the south coast and Bournemouth.

At Dean Court, he continued to score with great regularity and in July 1986, he moved to Southampton for £400,000. He played in eighty-two League games for the Saints, scoring thirty-six goals before signing for Queen's Park Rangers for £800,000.

25

A season later, Clarke arrived at Fratton Park for a club record fee of £415,000. The Newry-born Northern Ireland international who holds his country's scoring record made his debut against West Bromwich Albion in the opening game of the 1990–91 season. He topped the club's goal scoring charts that season with thirteen League goals including a hat-trick in the 4–1 win over Bristol City. He went on to score twenty-seven goals for Portsmouth in 107 first team appearances before retiring from the game.

CLARKE, IKE

After having scored thirty-nine League goals in 108 League appearances for West Bromwich Albion, Ike Clarke signed for Portsmouth for £7,000 in November 1947 and made a scoring debut in a 4–2 home defeat by Aston Villa.

The following season, which was Pompey's first League Championship winning season, the Tipton-born forward could not force his way into the team until November but in the twenty-four matches in which he did play, he scored fourteen goals.

In 1949–50 Pompey retained the title and Ike Clarke was the club's leading scorer in the League with seventeen goals and scored another three in the FA Cup. He reached double figures again in 1950–51 but then his scoring powers dwindled and in April 1952, he played his last game for the club. He had appeared in 129 games and scored fifty-eight goals.

In 1953 he left Fratton Park to become manager of Yeovil Town later moving to Kent, where he managed both Sittingbourne and Canterbury.

CLEAN SHEET

This is the colloquial expression to describe a goalkeeper's performance when he does not concede a goal. Alexander Kane in 1923–24 had twenty-five clean sheets from forty-two League appearances plus another two in the FA Cup competition. The next best is Alan Knight who kept twenty clean sheets in forty-two appearances in 1986–87 plus another four in various cup competitions.

COLOURS

Portsmouth came into being after a meeting held in the offices of Alderman J E Pink, a local solicitor. The club's first colours were salmon pink shirts with maroon collars and cuffs so they were quickly dubbed 'The Shrimps'.

In 1909 they changed their colours to white shirts with dark blue shorts and did so again before the start of the 1912–13 season. Pompey had just won promotion to the First Division of the Southern League and for their opening match at Brighton, wore royal blue shirts with white shorts.

Towards the end of the 1929–30 season, the club lost their now famous royal blue kit in a fire at the Fratton Park drying room and had to revert to the old salmon pink shirts for a friendly match at Bournemouth. The 1933–34 campaign began with Portsmouth wearing shirts of a slightly darker shade of blue and 1948–49 became the first full season for Pompey's famous red socks.

The club's change colours are red and black striped shirts, black shorts and red socks.

CONSECUTIVE HOME GAMES

Though Portsmouth played nine successive friendly matches at home in the wartime season of 1917–18, they did play an extraordinary sequence of six home games in succession in just twenty-five days (23 September–18 October 1899) winning all six games.

Date	Opponents	Competition	Result
23 September	Brighton United	Southern League	3–1
27 September	Chatham	South Dist Comb	4–0
30 September	Ryde	FA Cup	10–0
7 October	Bristol Rovers	Southern League	8–2
14 October	Cowes	FA Cup	3–2
18 October	Southampton	South Dist Comb	5–1

CONSECUTIVE SCORING

Jimmy Easson and Jack Weddle hold the club record for consecutive scoring in the Football League, being on target in six consecutive games.

Their records are:

Jimmy Easson 1931–32		Jack Weddle 1934–35	
Liverpool (Home 2–0)	2 goals	Preston N E (Home 4–0)	3 goals
Man City (Home 3–2)	2 goals	Tottenham H (Away 1–4)	1 goal
Man City (Away 3–3)	1 goal	Huddersfield (Home 5–0)	3 goals
Sheffield U (Home 2–1)	1 goal	Everton (Away 2–3)	1 goal
Blackburn R (Away 3–5)	3 goals	Derby County (Home 5–1)	1 goal
Derby County (Home 2–0)	1 goal	Aston Villa (Away 4–5)	2 goals

In the club's Southern League Division Two campaign of 1911–12, former Barnsley forward Harry Taylor made his debut in a 3–2 win over Cardiff, scoring the winning goal. From then until the end of the season, he scored in each of the eight matches, including six goals in a 7–0 win at Chesham.

COOK, FREDDIE

Signed from Newport County in April 1926, Welsh international winger Freddie Cook was one of Pompey's shrewdest signings. Making his debut on 1 May in the final match of the season, he scored one of the goals in a 4–0 win over Chelsea. An ever-present the following season when the club won promotion to the First Division, his crosses provided many of the openings from which Billy Haines scored his forty League goals.

Cook continued to be a regular in the Pompey line-up for seven seasons, scoring forty-two goals in 268 games before, at the end of the 1932–33 season, being released to join League of Ireland side, Waterford.

CORNER KICKS

On 5 December 1931, Portsmouth and Newcastle United made Football League history in the goal-less draw at St James' Park. The match watched by a crowd of 20,000 was the first without a single corner kick taking place.

COX, FREDDIE

Former Arsenal winger Freddie Cox lost his best years to the war, spending many of those years flying transport planes in the Far East. The Reading-born player later played an important role in getting the Gunners to two FA Cup Finals scoring valuable goals in the semi-finals of 1950 and 1952.

After a spell as player-coach and assistant manager at West Bromwich Albion, he became manager at Bournemouth, steering the Dean Court club to an excellent FA Cup run in 1957. He replaced Eddie Lever as Portsmouth manager in August 1958 but while in charge at Fratton Park had a difficult time. The club lost their First Division status in 1959 and were heading for the Third Division when in February 1961, he was sacked.

Cox later took Gillingham to the Fourth Division championship in 1963–64 and had a second spell managing Bournemouth before retiring to concentrate on his newsagent's business in the town.

CRICKETERS

Portsmouth have had eight players who have been cricketers of real note. Charles Burgess Fry, who played for Hampshire, Sussex and England, was one of the greatest all-rounders of his or any generation.

For Sussex he scored 20,656 runs at an average of 56.82 and for Hampshire, 3,829 at 58.90 runs. He captained England in Test matches and in 1901 scored six hundreds in consecutive first class innings to set a world record, subsequently equalled. In 1892 he established the world's long jump record of 23ft 5ins, a record that stood for twenty-one years. Although he only appeared in three first team games for Pompey in the 1902–03 season, he played for England against Ireland in 1901 and was at full-back for Southampton in the FA Cup Final of 1902.

George Frederick Wheldon, who appeared in sixty-three games for Pompey, was an England international and was a member of the Aston Villa side that did the 'double' in 1896–97. He was a good batsman and wicket-keeper and appeared for Worcestershire in both its second class and first class days, scoring 4,938 runs at an average of 22.55.

Arthur Mountenay hit six centuries in first class cricket, all for Leicestershire between 1911 and 1924, though he never quite established himself in the 1st XI. For Portsmouth he appeared in fifty-four games, scoring sixteen goals.

Arthur Egerton Knight was a legendary Pompey character who spent thirteen years on the club's books. He played many times for England's amateur international side and once for the full England side against Northern Ireland. He spent ten years on Hampshire's staff but only appeared in seven first class fixtures.

Stanley Shute Harris played cricket for Gloucestershire, Surrey and Sussex. A hard-hitting batsman, he played most of his cricket with Old Westminsters and Free Foresters. In 1904 he was captain of the Corinthians and was capped by England on six occasions. He appeared in just eight games for Portsmouth, scoring five goals including a hat-trick in a 5–0 win at Brighton.

Inside-forward Mike Barnard, who scored twenty-six goals in 123 League and Cup games for Portsmouth, represented Hampshire between 1952 and 1966. He was a handsome stroke maker and scored 9,314 runs at an average of 22.07 and a top score of 128 not out. He was also a specialist slip fielder and held 313 catches during his Hampshire career.

Ron Tindall was an excellent all-rounder who played for Surrey. Playing in 256 first class matches, he scored 5,383 runs at 24.69 and captured 150 wickets for 32.30 runs apiece. He appeared in 180 games for Pompey, later managing the club.

The last cricketer of note to play for the Fratton Park club was goalkeeper Jim Standen. Signed by Ron Tindall, he appeared in thirteen games before he retired from football. He played cricket for Worcestershire, taking 313 wickets at 25.35 runs each.

CROWD TROUBLE

Crowd disturbances are far from a modern phenomenon at major football matches. Behaviour at Fratton Park has usually been of a high standard. Although Pompey's supporters are well renowned for voicing their opinions at suspect referees, the occasions when their demonstrations boil over beyond the verbal are very rare indeed.

However one such occasion did take place on 27 August 1983 when Pompey entertained Middlesbrough on the opening day of the season following their promotion to the Second Division the previous season. The visitors won 1–0 with a controversial goal scored while Alan Knight lay concussed in his goalmouth.

When the final whistle went, determined troublemakers invaded the field of play, proving that higher fences would be needed to contain the hooligan element. Chairman John Deacon immediately instituted life bans against fans convicted of causing trouble at Fratton Park.

Away from Portsmouth, the club's match at Swindon on 30 January 1904 was interrupted by crowd trouble. Matt Reilly, Pompey's Northern Ireland international was so incensed at being bombarded with clinker by the home fans that he went out and hit one of them – an incident which earned the popular Irishman a two week suspension.

In March 1919, Pompey played Harland and Wolfe in a friendly match at the Dell. On the final whistle, there was a fierce outbreak of fighting between supporters of both sides and the referee was chased to the dressing room by a very angry crowd.

CUNLIFFE, DANNY

Danny Cunliffe became the club's first full England international when he played for England against Northern Ireland on 17 March 1900. The Bolton-born forward played his early football with Bolton Juniors before joining Oldham County and then Liverpool.

He joined Portsmouth in 1899 and appeared in the club's first fixture at Chatham which Pompey won 1–0. Three days later, on 5 September 1899, he scored one of the goals in a 2–0 win over Southampton in the first match to be played at Fratton Park.

When Pompey won the Southern League title in 1901–02, Cunliffe was top scorer with eighteen goals, including four in a 5–0 win at Watford. He also led the way with thirteen goals as the club won the Western League Championship that season, including a hat-trick in a 5–0 victory over Queen's Park Rangers.

In 1902–03, Cunliffe scored twenty two goals to be the club's leading scorer, a feat he also achieved in the next two seasons. He scored 178 goals in 306 games for the Fratton Park club before later playing for New Brighton Tower and New Brompton.

31

D

DAVIES, REG

Right-half Reg Davies joined Pompey from Sutton Town in 1922 and made his debut in a 1–0 win over Reading in October of that year. He was impressive in the twenty one games he played that season and soon established himself as a first team regular, in 1923–24 playing an important part in the club winning the Third Division (South) championship. He missed just one game the following season, a 5–0 defeat at Hull City.

In 1926–27 Reg Davies was one of seven ever-presents as Pompey finished as runners-up in the Second Division to win promotion to the top flight for the first time in their history. He scored the winner at Bradford City in a 2–1 win and was one of the scorers in the club's 9–1 defeat of Notts County. He played the last of his 216 first team games in the 6–2 defeat at Leicester City in February 1928 before joining Brentford.

DAVIES, RON

Holywell-born Ron Davies began his footballing career at Chester, where he was made to hurdle wearing army boots during training, an exercise he later claimed gave him extra power when jumping for crosses. After spells with Luton Town and Norwich City, Southampton signed him for a record £55,000.

He was already a Welsh international and scored thirty-seven goals in forty-one First Division games to top the goalscoring charts. His heading powers were awesome and in a seven-year career at the Dell he scored 134 goals in 240 League appearances.

Davies was signed by Portsmouth in the summer of 1973. He appeared in all the club's fifty competitive matches the following season, scoring sixteen goals. He had played in a further nineteen League and Cup games in 1974–75 when Manchester United took him to Old Trafford for £25,000. Unfortunately for their supporters, his powers were waning and he registered only eight substitute appearances without scoring.

DEATH

Frank Bedingfield, who replaced Sandy Brown when the latter joined Tottenham Hotspur, top-scored for Pompey in 1900–01 with thirty goals, his only full season with the club.

The following season he had scored another twenty-seven goals but after scoring the only goal in the FA Cup win over Reading, he collapsed in the dressing room. Consumption was diagnosed, and although money was raised to send him to convalesce in South Africa, Bedingfield died at the age of twenty seven in November 1904.

One of the club's reserve wingers died in tragic circumstances. Scottish-born Duncan Gilchrist collapsed and died after heading a ball in a match against Gosport in April 1924.

Portsmouth's centre-half, Bob Kearney who played in sixty-five games in seasons 1929–30 and 1930–31 was taken ill with pneumonia. Five days later he was dead.

An unusual accident resulted in the death of one of the Pompey youngsters. Jackie Ambler suffered severe stomach injuries during a match in October 1959 when he was hit by the ball from close range. Three months later he died after an operation.

DEBUTS

There have been a number of goal scoring debuts for Pompey. One that deserves special mention was on 21 March 1959 when sixteen year old youth team forward Jimmy White became the club's youngest First Division debutant and scored in a 1–1 draw against Birmingham City.

DEFEATS: FEWEST

During the 1921–22 season, Portsmouth went through the forty-two match programme suffering only seven defeats to finish third in Division Three. Two seasons later they again only suffered seven setbacks but this time were rewarded with the Third Division championship.

DEFEATS – MOST

Portsmouth's total of 27 defeats during the 1958–59 season is the worst in the club's history. Not surprisingly they finished bottom of the First Division and were relegated.

DEFEATS – WORST

Portsmouth's record defeat in the Football League was when Leicester City beat them 10–0 in a First Division game at Filbert Street on 20 October 1928. Pompey were also beaten 10–0 by Tottenham Hotspur in a London Combination game on 31 March 1917.

DEFENSIVE RECORDS

Portsmouth's best defensive record was established in 1986–87 and helped the club win promotion from the Second Division. They conceded just twenty-eight goals in that campaign, with goalkeeper Alan Knight keeping twenty clean sheets. Pompey's worst defensive record was in 1958–59 when they let in 112 goals to finish bottom of the First Division.

DICKINSON, JIMMY

One of the greatest names in British football is Jimmy Dickinson. He holds the club appearance record with 834 first team matches and another thirty-one wartime games. He is also second to Swindon Town's John Trollope (770) with most postwar Football League appearances for one club with 764.

It was 1943 when Dickinson was discovered by his schoolteacher, Eddie Lever, later to become Pompey manager. He played in a trial game against Reading in May 1943 and eight months later signed professional forms for the Fratton Park club. He made his Football League debut for the club on 31 August 1946 in a 3–1 win over Blackburn Rovers at home.

Almost faultless in defence, Dickinson was instrumental in the club winning its first League Championship in 1948–49 and at the end of that season he won the first of forty-eight international caps for England when they defeated Norway 4–1 in Oslo. Pompey retained the title the following season with Dickinson again in commanding form. In June 1950 he played in the World Cup Finals in Brazil and was a member of the England team humiliated 1–0 by USA.

In November 1950, Dickinson scored his first League goal for the club in a 3–3 draw at home to Charlton Athletic.The summer of 1954 saw him playing in his second World Cup Finals in Switzerland but unfortunately in the match against Belgium, which ended 4–4, he scored the first own goal of his career. He played the last of his forty-eight internationals in December 1956 against Denmark at Molineux, England winning 5–2.

Dickinson had an almost telepathic understanding of Jimmy Scoular's attacking instincts and Jack Froggatt owed much of his success to the service he received from the Alton-born defender. He was an ever-present for seven of his nineteen seasons of League football, twice playing in runs of more than 100 consecutive League matches.

He was awarded the MBE in the Queen's Birthday Honours of 1964 and played his last game for the club on 24 April 1965, helping Pompey avoid relegation by drawing 1–1 at Northampton. He then took up a full-time post as Portsmouth's public relations officer and three years later became the club secretary. In May 1977 he took over from Ian St John as Pompey manager and relegation was avoided.

On 30 March 1979, on reaching the dressing room following a 1–1 draw at home to Barnsley, Dickinson collapsed with a massive heart attack and was rushed into intensive care. Despite making a recovery, he resigned as Portsmouth manager in August of that year and took up the position of chief executive. Sadly, the legendary Pompey player suffered another heart attack and on 8 November 1982 at the age of fifty-seven, he died. A private cremation was followed by a Memorial Service to Gentleman Jim.

DILLON, KEVIN

His Football League career began with Birmingham City where much of his time at St Andrews was spent on the left-wing, from where he scored some stunning goals, with either curling shots or after a mazy dribble. Dillon, a player with silky skills, had a suspect temperament and was often in trouble with referees for back-chatting.

This did not deter Pompey and in March 1983 they paid £140,000 for the midfield player's services. He made his debut in the 1–0 home defeat of Bristol Rovers and in the eleven games he played at the end of the 1983–84 Third Division promotion-winning season, scored five goals. Two of these were penalties in a 2–2 draw against Reading.

He was a regular over the next six seasons, playing in 249 League and Cup games before returning to his native north-east to play for Newcastle United, later ending his career with Reading.

DISMISSALS

The first Portsmouth player to be sent off was Roderick Walker, a full-back who had joined the club from Motherwell. He got his marching orders in Pompey's 2–1 home defeat against Bristol Rovers on 7 January 1905.

In Portsmouth's first season in the Football League, right-half Ernie Thompson, who scored one of the goals in Pompey's 3–0 win over Sheffield United, was sent off. He was, however, recalled after players from both sides had appealed to the referee – an incident over which both clubs were cautioned by the League.

DOYLE, BOB

Dumbarton-born midfielder Bob Doyle began his Football League career with Barnsley, scoring sixteen goals in 149 League games between 1972 and 1975. The tough-tackling Scot then joined Peterborough United before moving to Blackpool. It was from the Bloomfield Road club that Portsmouth signed him in December 1980 and he made his debut in a 1–0 defeat at Sheffield United.

In 1982–83 when Pompey were promoted as champions of the Third

Division, Doyle played in forty-four games, scoring just one goal, from the penalty spot in a 1–1 draw at Oxford United. He played in 194 games for the Fratton Park club before leaving to end his League career with Hull City.

DRAWS

Portsmouth played their greatest number of drawn League matches in a single season in 1981–82 when nineteen of their matches ended all square and their fewest in 1928–29 when only six of their matches were drawn.

The club's highest scoring draw is 4–4, a scoreline in nine League games: Bolton Wanderers (Home 1928–29) Chelsea (Away 1932–33) Liverpool (Away 1938–39) Preston North End (Home 1946–47) Blackpool (Home 1953–54) Sheffield Wednesday (Away 1953–54) Chelsea (Home 1955–56) Tottenham Hotspur (Away 1958–59) and Fulham (Home 1984–85).

E

EASSON, JIMMY

Brechin-born Jimmy Easson was an inside-left who joined Portsmouth from Dundee in 1928. Though he made his debut in a goal-less draw against Manchester United in the final game of the 1928–29 season, it was the following season before he began to establish himself in the side.

An ever-present in 1930–31, he also top scored with 29 League goals, including hat-tricks against Manchester United (Home 4–1) and Liverpool (Home 4–0).

It was his goalscoring feats that season that led to him winning his first cap for Scotland against Austria in Vienna in May 1931. His second came a week later in Geneva when he scored once in a 3–2 victory over Switzerland. His third and, surprisingly, his final cap was against Wales in

Cardiff in October 1933. Easson also won a runners-up medal after Pompey were beaten by Manchester City in the FA Cup Final of 1934. He played for Pompey for eleven seasons, scoring 107 League and Cup goals in 312 appearances before in March 1939 he joined Fulham.

He left Craven Cottage a few years later and returned to Fratton Park where he became one of the club's trainers when Pompey won the First Division championship two years in succession.

EIRE

The first Portsmouth player to be capped by the Republic of Ireland was Jimmy McAlinden who played against Portugal on 16 June 1946. The most capped player is Eoin Hand who won twenty caps playing for his country.

ELLIS, PETER

Local-born Peter Ellis, a fiercely competitive defender, made his debut in the final game of the 1973–74 season in a 2–0 home defeat by Nottingham Forest. He went on to win a regular place in the Pompey line up and by the time the club won promotion from the Fourth Division in 1979–80, Ellis at the age of twenty-four, was the club's longest serving player.

He went on to appear in 246 League games, scoring just one goal, which came in the 2–1 win over Brentford in December 1982.

Just before the start of the 1983–84 season, Ellis at first refused the club's offer of a new contract but eventually accepted it and it proved to be his last season at Fratton Park. He joined Southend United in the close season and appeared in twelve League games for the Roots Hall club.

EVER-PRESENTS

There have been forty-eight Portsmouth players who have been ever-presents throughout a Football League season. The greatest number of ever-present seasons by a Portsmouth player is seven by Jimmy Dickinson. Next in line is goalkeeper Alan Knight with six seasons.

F

FA CUP

Portsmouth first participated in the FA Cup on 30 September 1899 when they beat Cowes 10–0 in a qualifying round match. Since then they have gone on to win the trophy in 1939, although their first appearance in a final was in 1929 when they lost 2–0 to Bolton Wanderers.

FA CUP FINALS

Portsmouth have appeared in three FA Cup Finals, winning the trophy on just one occasion:

1929	Bolton Wanderers (Wembley)	Lost 0–2
1934	Manchester City (Wembley)	Lost 1–2
1939	Wolverhampton Wanderers (Wembley)	Won 4–1

In the final of 1939, Portsmouth took the lead in the thirty-first minute when former Wolves' player Barlow placed a rising ball with pace and accuracy beyond Scott's reach. Two minutes before half time, Stan Cullis was beaten by the bounce of Worrall's centre and Anderson put Pompey 2–0 up.

The third goal, thirty seconds into the second half was scored by Parker who followed up Barlow's shot that had been parried by Scott. Dorsett then pulled a goal back for Wolves to make it 3–1. Pompey's fourth and final goal of the match came in the sixty-seventh minute when Worrall floated over an accurate cross for Parker to head home with the Wolves' defence flat-footed. So Portsmouth had won the Cup at the third attempt and captain Jimmy Guthrie collected the trophy from King George VI.

The Portsmouth side was: H.Walker; L.Morgan; W.Rochford; J.Guthrie; T.Rowe; G.Wharton; F.Worrall; J.McAlinden; J.Anderson; H.Barlow and C.Parker.

Jimmy Guthrie holds the FA Cup aloft after Pompey's 1939 triumph.

FA CUP SEMI-FINALS

Portsmouth have participated in five FA Cup semi-finals up to the end of the 1996–97 season, with the last occasion being against Liverpool in 1991–92. In this match, Pompey drew 1–1 with the Anfield side at Highbury and then 0–0 at Villa Park before losing 3–1 on penalties.

FENWICK, TERRY

Although he was born in the north-east, it was Crystal Palace who recognised his potential and after winning England Youth honours, Terry Venables signed him to his first professional contract.

Fenwick made his League debut against Spurs in December 1977 and in two years at Selhurst Park, won three England Under-21 caps and helped Palace to the Second Division title.

He followed Venables to Queen's Park Rangers, where he played against Spurs in the FA Cup Final of 1982. As a member of Rangers' Second Division championship team of 1983, he followed Venables again to White Hart Lane in December 1987. By this time, he had won nineteen full England caps and added another in February 1988 by going on as a substitute against Israel.

Although signed principally as a central defender, Fenwick's versatility saw him play at full-back, in central defence, in midfield and in a continental style sweeper's role. He broke a leg in a Littlewoods Cup match at Old Trafford in October 1989 and within a month of making a full recovery, he broke an ankle in the pre-match warm up for an FA Cup tie at Portsmouth.

In February 1995 he became Portsmouth's manager and after finishing 21st at the end of the 1995–96 season, he led the club to the verge of the play-offs the following season.

FERRIER, HARRY

Full-back Harry Ferrier was on Barnsley's books when he 'guested' for Portsmouth during the Second World War, having appeared for Arsenal, Brentford, Chelsea, Clapton Orient, Crystal Palace, Fulham, Middlesbrough, Millwall, Queen's Park Rangers, Spurs and Watford in a similar capacity.

He soon made the move permanent and made the first of 257 senior appearances in eight years in a 3–1 win over Blackburn Rovers on the opening day of the 1946–47 season. Missing just the last two games of the 1948–49 season, which were both defeats, he was an ever-present the following season in which Pompey retained the First Division championship they had won for the first time the previous season.

In May 1954, he left Fratton Park to become player-manager at Gloucester City.

FEWEST DEFEATS

During Portsmouth's Third Division championship winning season of 1923–24, the club went through the forty-two match programme losing only seven games, a feat they first achieved in 1921–22. The first of these defeats came in the fourth game of the season at Newport County (1–2) whilst the only club to do the 'double' over Pompey were Millwall who won 1–0 at The Den on Christmas Day and 2–0 at Fratton Park on Boxing Day.

FIRST DIVISION

Portsmouth have had two spells in the First Division. Promoted in 1926–27, the club drew their first ever match in the top flight, 3–3 at Sunderland with Cook, Mackie and Haines the scorers. At the end of the season, Pompey finished twentieth, just avoiding relegation by one point. They battled against relegation again the following season, again finishing in twentieth place.

In 1930–31 Pompey finished fourth in the First Division, their highest pre-war position.

Following the resumption of the game after the Second World War, Pompey had two seasons of finishing in mid-table before winning the First Division Championship for the first time in 1948–49. Finishing five points ahead of Manchester United, Pompey won 5–0 at Everton and Newcastle United, whilst at Fratton Park they were unbeatable, winning eighteen and drawing three of their home fixtures.

The club retained the title in 1949–50, winning the Championship on goal average from Wolverhampton Wanderers. They had become the first club since Huddersfield Town in 1923–24 to win on goal average and the first since Sheffield Wednesday in 1929–30 to successfully defend their title. Everton were again one of the teams to suffer as Pompey beat them 7–0 at Fratton Park with Duggie Reid netting a hat-trick.

The club's first spell of twenty-five seasons in the First Division ended in 1958–59 when they finished bottom of the top flight after coming close to relegation the previous season.

Pompey's second and last spell of top flight football lasted just one season, 1987–88. Going down 4–2 at the Manor Ground to Oxford United in the opening match of the season, they never really came to terms with First Division football and finished seven points adrift of Chelsea in nineteenth place.

FIRST LEAGUE MATCH

Portsmouth's first Football League match was a Third Division game against Swansea Town at Fratton Park on 28 August 1920. Pompey won 3–0 with Stringfellow, Reid and James the goalscorers.

The Portsmouth team was: Robson; Probert; Potts; Abbott; Harwood; Turner; Thompson; Stringfellow; Reid; James and Beedie.

FIRST MATCH

Pompey's first match was a Southern League game at Chatham on 2 September 1899. A goal from winger Harry 'Nobby' Clarke gave the club a 1–0 win. The Portsmouth side in that historic opening fixture was: Reilly; H.Turner; Wilkie; Blyth; Stringfellow; Cleghorn; Marshall; Cunliffe; A.Brown; B.Smith; and Clarke. They were quickly named 'The Shrimps' as they were wearing salmon pink shirts with maroon collars and cuffs.

FLEWIN, REG

Centre-half Reg Flewin joined Portsmouth from Ryde Sports on the Isle of Wight and made his first team debut in a 2–1 win over Grimsby Town in May 1939, eighteen months after he had signed for the club. His playing career was badly affected by the war and though he appeared in 202 wartime games for Pompey, he only played in 169 League and Cup games in eighteen years at the club.

He wasPompey's regular centre-half after the war and although a serious injury put him out of the side in January 1951, he had gained two League Championship medals as captain. He appeared for England in a wartime international and went on two FA tours to Canada in 1950 and Australia in 1951.

He retired from playing in 1953 and after a spell as youth team coach, became the club's assistant manager. In October 1960, he left Fratton Park after twenty three years to become his own boss with Stockport County. He later managed Bournemouth and almost took the Dean Court club to promotion to the Second Division in 1964.

FLOODLIGHTS

Pompey played their first floodlight match on 22 October 1951 against Southampton at The Dell. The Saints in return visited Fratton Park on 2 March 1953 as Portsmouth played their first game under their newly installed floodlights.

On 22 February 1956, Portsmouth entertained Newcastle United at Fratton Park in the first Football League game to be played under floodlights. The evening was almost a disaster for one hour before kick-off the lights failed and, on a bitterly cold night, both teams had to change by candlelight. Power was eventually restored and the game kicked off ten minutes late, with the Magpies running out winners 2–0.

During the summer of 1962, the original roof-mounted floodlights were replaced by the existing pylons. The new 120ft high floodlight towers cost £14,000 and were a gift from the Supporters' Club. They were officially 'opened' in October of that year with a friendly match against Burnley.

FOOTBALL LEAGUE

Portsmouth joined the Third Division of the Football League in 1920 after 17 seasons of playing in the Southern League.

44

FOOTBALL LEAGUE CUP

Sad to relate, Portsmouth have failed to make much of an impact upon the Football League (later Milk, Littlewoods, Rumbelows and Coca Cola) Cup.

Introduced in season 1960–61, Pompey were given a bye in the first round before goals from Saunders and Priscott gave them a 2–0 win over Coventry City. It was Ron Saunders who scored both Pompey goals in the third round as Manchester City were also beaten 2–0. Chelsea were beaten by a Jimmy White goal in the fourth round as Pompey progressed to the quarter-finals. Drawn away to Rotherham United, Pompey crashed 3–0 and did not reach the same stage of the competition again until 1993–94.

In 1961–62, Harold Middleton scored all four goals in Pompey's 4–2 second round replay win over Derby County and the following season, Ron Saunders netted a hat-trick in a 5–1 win over Brighton and Hove Albion.

Pompey's heaviest defeat in the competition came in 1981–82 when they lost 5–0 at Loftus Road in a second round first leg tie against Queen's Park Rangers. The club's biggest win in the competition is also 5–0, a score line inflicted upon Rotherham United at Fratton Park after a second round first leg goal-less draw at Millmoor. Goals from Durnin and Walsh helped beat Swindon Town 2–0 in round three before a goal by Bjorn Kristensen was enough to defeat Peterborough United after a goal-less draw at London Road. Two goals from Paul Walsh gave Pompey a superb 2–2 draw against Manchester United at Old Trafford but despite a good performance in the replay at Fratton Park, a Brian McClair goal put Pompey out of the competition.

Portsmouth's record to date in the Football League Cup (correct to July 1997) is as follows:

P	W	D	L	F	A
134	56	27	51	188	177

FORMATION

At a meeting on 5 April 1898, held in the High Street, Portsmouth offices of solicitor Alderman J E Pink, six business and professional men agreed to buy some ground close to Goldsmith Avenue for £4,950 which they

developed into Fratton Park in record breaking time. A team of professional footballers was signed up by manager Frank Brettell, one of the most
respected men in football and entry to the Southern League obtained for
the new club's September 1899 kick-off.

FOSTER, STEVE

A product of the Pompey Youth side, Steve Foster made his first team
debut during 1975–76 when the club finished bottom of the Second
Division. He established himself as a first team regular the following season and scored his first goal for the club in a 3–1 win at Tranmere Rovers.

Foster had arrived at Fratton Park as a centre-forward but had been converted into a centre-half by manager Ian St John. He played in 127 League
and Cup games for Pompey before being sold to Brighton and Hove
Albion for £15,000 in the summer of 1979.

At the Goldstone Ground he won full international honours, being
capped three times by England, and was instrumental in the club reaching
the FA Cup Final, where they lost to Manchester United after a replay.

He then joined Aston Villa in March 1984 but by the end of the year he
had been transferred to Luton Town. He played in 212 games for the
Kenilworth Road club before moving to Oxford United, his fifth League
club in the summer of 1989.

He returned to Brighton for a second spell in August 1992 but after playing in a total of 330 games for the Seagulls, was released following knee
ligament damage that required surgery.

FOURTH DIVISION

Portsmouth have had just one spell of two seasons in the Fourth Division.
When bottom of the Third Division in 1977–78, Pompey were relegated to
the League's basement.

They lost their first match in the Fourth Division 1–0 at home to
Bradford City and then went down 5–2 at York City. A draw at Hartlepool
was followed by a run of six matches in which the club only dropped one
point. Peter Mellor, the Pompey 'keeper, kept a clean sheet in each of those
six matches.

Towards the end of the year, Pompey were in second place with manager Jimmy Dickinson winning November's Manager of the Month award. Sadly, on 30 March 1979 he collapsed with a massive heart attack and was rushed into intensive care. The club had by then started to slip and ended their first season in the Fourth Division in seventh place.

In 1979–80, Pompey finished fourth and were promoted to the Third Division. Frank Burrows had taken over as manager and one of his first signings was Swindon Town's Steve Aizlewood. The Portsmouth manager also made a number of other signings, with Joe Laidlaw from Doncaster Rovers for £15,000, being one of the best.

The club made their best start since the Second World War, winning all of their first five matches, including a 6–1 victory over Scunthorpe United. Despite injuries to key players, Portsmouth were in fourth place with just four games to play when they only drew 1–1 at home to lowly Crewe Alexandra. They then beat Halifax Town and Peterborough United but still had to win at Northampton Town to ensure promotion. Even so, they needed Walsall and Peterborough to beat Newport and Bradford. Pompey beat the Cobblers 2–0, but Newport surprisingly beat Walsall and so with Peterborough beating Bradford 1–0, the Fratton Park club were promoted with having a wider goal difference margin.

FRATTON PARK

Following the decision to form a professional club, a limited company was set up in 1898 and for £4,950 it bought a market garden near Fratton railway station. A further £16,000 was spent on laying a pitch and building a short South Stand with seats and also laying a full length North Cover for standing.

Fratton Park was one of five grounds opened during the first week of September 1899 and hosted its first match on 5 September – a friendly against Southampton.

Six years later, the club's success in the Southern League prompted the building of a mock-Tudor pavilion at the Frogmore Road entrance to the ground, linked to The Pompey pub behind and with a balcony that overlooked the playing surface.

Following Portsmouth's elevation to the Football League and their subsequent promotion to the Second Division, they commissioned a new South Stand. It was designed by Archibald Leitch and was officially opened by League President John McKenna on 25 August 1925. The stand, which had 4,000 seats, a paddock below and a balcony of criss-cross structures in blue on a white background, cost £12,000.

Following promotion to the First Division, appearances in two FA Cup Finals and the sale of Jimmy Allen to Aston Villa, the club built the North Stand during the 1934–35 season. At one stage it was even called the Jimmy Allen Stand.

After the war, the club's floodlights were switched on for the first time in March 1953 but were not used for a League game until 22 February 1956 when Newcastle United were the visitors. In fact, this was the very first League game to be played under lights. Six years later, the floodlights were replaced by the club's existing pylons.

Over the next two decades or so, Fratton Park hardly changed but between 1988 and 1993 more than £4 million was spent on a major refurbishment programme. The Fratton End was found to have deteriorated seriously and was demolished, leaking roofs were recovered and old barriers replaced. Also new changing rooms, offices and lounges were fitted out.

Former Queen's Park Rangers chairman Jim Gregory bought Pompey for £2 million and soon unveiled plans for a £10 million stadium on the railway goods yard adjacent to Fratton Park. However, it soon became clear that this plan would not work because British Railways had other ideas for the site.

The club then sat down with the local council in an attempt to find alternative sites. However, the demands of the Taylor Report and the restrictions imposed by the planners, brought conflict.

In April 1993, the club unveiled their 'Parkway Stadium' plan but this met with objections from a number of areas and six months later, the council's planning committee turned down the scheme. A month later, after the plans had been amended, they were shown to the full council and accepted by twenty votes to nineteen. After a public inquiry, the plans were called in by the Secretary of State and in December 1994, the Department of the Environment inspector threw the scheme out.

Pompey then decided to redevelop Fratton Park with major refurbishments and a brand new 4,750-seater Fratton End. The £2.5 million revamp seems the best option available to the club at the moment, but they certainly have not given up on their plans to build a new 25,000 all-seater stadium.

FROGGATT, JACK

Born in Sheffield, Jack Froggatt's family had football connections, in that his father played before the Second World War for Sheffield Wednesday and his second cousin, Redfern Froggatt also signed for his local club and played in 434 games for the Owls.

Froggatt was still in the Royal Air Force when he got a trial with Pompey. He signed for the club as a centre-half, scoring on his debut in the War League South game against Southampton before later managing to persuade Jack Tinn to play him at outside-left.

He made his Football League debut in a 2–0 defeat at Derby County after missing the opening game of the 1946–47 season, the only one he missed. In 1947–48 he scored his first hat-trick for the club in a 6–0 win over Sheffield United. He was an important member of the Pompey side that won the League Championships in 1948–49 and 1949–50 and he won the first of thirteen international caps against Northern Ireland at Maine Road in 1949, scoring a goal in a 9–2 win.

When he joined Second Division Leicester City in March 1954 he had scored seventy-one goals in 304 League and Cup appearances for the Fratton Park club.

FULL MEMBERS' CUP

Originally called the Full Members' Cup because it was open only to First and Second Division clubs, Portsmouth's first match saw them beat Charlton Athletic at Fratton Park 4–1 with Paul Wood scoring two of the

49

goals. In the next round, Pompey travelled to Stamford Bridge, but were beaten 3–0 by a strong Chelsea side who went on to beat Manchester City in the final.

In 1986–87, Portsmouth had a good run in the competition. After beating Crystal Palace 4–0 in the first round, a Kevin Dillon hat-trick helped them defeat Millwall 3–2 after extra time. Round three saw them travel to Hillsborough, where a Vince Hilaire goal gave Pompey a 1–0 win. Drawn away again in round four, the club gave a good account of themselves but went down 3–1 to Norwich City.

G

GILFILLAN, JOCK

Goalkeeper Jock Gilfillan began his career with East Fife before joining Hearts, from whom Pompey signed him in December 1928. He was ever-present in 1929–30, 1930–31 and 1931–32 and made 158 consecutive League appearances after missing just one of his first season's games.

Described as one of the safest goalkeepers in the Football League, Gilfillan made the last of his 360 appearances for Portsmouth in a 5–1 defeat against Arsenal at Fratton Park on 12 December 1936.

At the end of that season, he joined Queen's Park Rangers, taking with him the unique record of having played in both Scottish and English Cup finals. Gilfillan was three times a loser, playing for East Fife in 1927 and Pompey in 1929 and 1934.

GOALKEEPERS

Portsmouth FC has almost always been extremely well served by its goalkeepers and most of them have been highly popular with the supporters. Their first outstanding 'keeper was Matt Reilly, an Irish goalkeeper already known to the Portsmouth public, having played for the Royal Artillery. He was capped twice by his country against England and played in 258 games for Pompey between 1899 and 1904 before leaving to play for Dundee.

Ned Robson was Pompey's 'keeper during their first season of League football. A most dependable custodian, he missed just one of the club's first seventy-five League games before suffering a serious hand injury in a match at Southampton in March 1922. He never played for Portsmouth again and at the end of the season, signed for Sunderland for £150.

Alex Kane was signed from Hearts and appeared in ninety-six consecutive League games after making his debut in a 2–1 win at Plymouth. He holds the club record for the most clean sheets in a season with twenty-five in 1923–24. He lost his place to Dan McPhail who played a decisive part in the club's promotion to the First Division in 1926–27, saving four of the five penalties awarded against the club.

Another former Hearts 'keeper, Jock Gilfillan, joined Pompey in 1928 and gave great service, appearing in 360 League and Cup games and the FA Cup Finals of 1929 and 1934.

Ernie Butler who joined Portsmouth as an eighteen year old from Bath City, played in 240 League and Cup games between 1946 and 1953 and was ever-present during the club's League Championship successes of 1948–49 and 1949–50. He was followed by Northern Ireland international Norman Uprichard, signed from Swindon Town and one of the bravest 'keepers ever to turn out for the Fratton Park club. He played in 195 first team games during a Pompey career hampered by injuries.

John Milkins missed very few games for Pompey after establishing himself as first choice in 1965. A safe handler of the ball, he played in 389 League and Cup games for the club, being an ever-present in 1968–69.

Pompey's current 'keeper is Alan Knight. He has given great service to the club and in 1995–96 passed Peter Bonetti's League record of goalscoring appearances for one club. He has appeared in 751 first team games, although he is still 123 League appearances short of beating Jimmy Dickinson's club record.

GOAL AVERAGE

Portsmouth had to win the last match of the 1949–50 season against Aston Villa to retain their First Division title. Pompey were forced to use Bill Thompson at centre-forward as deputy for the injured Ike Clarke. It was

Thompson's first match for the first team as a forward, though he had played at full-back, wing-half and centre-half. Wolves were playing Birmingham City, who had already been relegated and were hoping that Pompey would drop a point and that they could then win the title themselves.

At half time Portsmouth led 2–0, with Thompson scoring inside the first minute, but news came through from Molineux that Wolves were 5–0 up. Pompey went on to win 5–1 with Thompson scoring another goal, and Wolves 6–1. Both teams had fifty-three points but Pompey became the first team since Huddersfield Town in 1923–24 to win the championship on goal average. Portsmouth's goal average was 1.947, while Wolves' was 1.551.

GOALS

The most goals Portsmouth have ever scored in one game was their 16–1 victory over Clapton Orient at Fratton Park in a London War League game on 28 February 1942. In the Football League, Notts County were beaten 9–1 in a Second Division game on 9 April 1927.

GOALS: CAREER BEST

The highest goal scorer in the club's history is Peter Harris, who between season 1946–47 and the end of season 1959–60, netted 208 goals for Pompey – 193 in the League and fifteen in the FA Cup. On top of this, he scored twenty-four goals during the League South Cup matches of 1944–45 and 1945–46.

GOALS: INDIVIDUAL

Only two Portsmouth players have scored five goals in a League game. The first was Alf Strange as Pompey beat Gillingham 6–1 in a Third Division game on 27 January 1923. The feat was equalled by the club's highest goal scorer, Peter Harris, who scored all five goals in a 5–2 win over Aston Villa in a First Division game at Fratton Park on 3 September 1958.

A number of Portsmouth players have scored four goals in a League game – Henry Havelock (Nottingham Forest 5–1, 1925–26); Billy Haines (Preston North End 5–1, 1926–27); Peter Harris (Sheffield United 6–2, 1954–55); Ray Hiron (Norwich City 5–2, 1968–69); and Guy Whittingham (Bristol Rovers 4–1, 1992–93). Whittingham also scored four goals in Pompey's 5–1 FA Cup win over Bournemouth in 1990–91.

During the Second World War, Andy Black of Hearts and Scotland scored eight goals as Pompey beat Clapton Orient 16–1 in a London War League game. Also that season, he scored four goals in a 7–2 win over Charlton.

Herbert Barlow scored six goals in Pompey's 10–2 win over Bournemouth in a Football League South game in 1940–41, emulating Jimmy Taylor's feat in a 7–0 win over Chesham in 1911–12.

During the First World War, Joseph Turner scored five goals in a match for Pompey on three occasions, whilst Danny Cunliffe scored four goals on two occasions for Portsmouth in Southern League games.

GOALS: SEASON

The club's highest League goalscorer in any one season is Guy Whittingham who scored 42 League goals as Portsmouth finished third in the First Division in 1992–93. He also holds the season's highest tally for all matches with forty-seven goals in that campaign, scoring two in the League Cup and three in the Anglo-Italian Cup.

GORDON, JOHNNY

An all-action forward, Johnny Gordon was very much the Pompey fans favourite. He signed as an apprentice at Fratton Park from the local Hillside Youth Club in 1947 and after turning professional, made his League debut against Blackpool in August 1951.

By 1953–54, he had become a regular in the Pompey side. Often the scorer of two goals in a match – a feat he achieved on ten occasions – he scored just one hat-trick. That came in a 4–4 draw against Sheffield Wednesday at Hillsborough when Pompey went in at half time 2–0 down.

Birmingham City, keen to acquire a proven goal score, signed him for £10,000 in September 1958 and he marked his debut for the St Andrews

Club with a goal. He continued to be a regular marksman for Birmingham, scoring forty goals in 115 first team games before the lure of his home town team proved too strong and in March 1961 he returned to Fratton Park.

In his second spell, he helped Pompey win the Third Division championship in 1962. He appeared in 489 first team games, scoring 120 goals, and played his last game for the club at Huddersfield in May 1967

GREGORY, JOHN

Known as 'Mr Versatility' during his playing days, John Gregory appeared in nine different positions during his time with Aston Villa. He was the winner of six England caps and appeared in the FA Cup Final of 1982 for Queen's Park Rangers and won a Second Division championship medal with Derby County after scoring some vital goals for the Rams.

Gregory was appointed Portsmouth's player-coach in August 1988, and took over as manager five months later. However, after fifty weeks in charge, he was sacked after a poor run, thus gaining the dubious distinction of being the shortest serving Pompey manager.

GUEST PLAYERS

The 'guest' system was used by all the clubs during the two wars. Although at times it was abused almost beyond belief (in that some sides that opposed Portsmouth had ten or eleven 'guests') it normally worked sensibly and effectively to the benefit of players, clubs and supporters alike.

The most distinguished players to 'guest' for Pompey were England internationals Ted Drake of Arsenal, who scored four goals in a 9–1 win over Crystal Palace in his only game for the club and Manchester United's John Aston. The Hearts and Scotland forward Andy Black played in fifty-two League and Cup games for Pompey during the Second World War, scoring sixty-six goals including eight in the 16–0 win over Clapton Orient.

Other international players to 'guest' for Portsmouth included Jimmy Allen (Aston Villa and England), Peter Buchanan (Chelsea and England),

Frank Mitchell (Birmingham City and England), Alec Massie (Chelsea and Scotland), John Jackson (Chelsea and Scotland) and James Mason (Third Lanark and Scotland).

GUNTER, PHIL

Local-born defender Phil Gunter made the first of his 359 League and Cup appearances for Pompey in a 3–1 win over Newcastle United on 27 October 1951, although it was 1955–56 before he fully established himself in the side.

Though he only missed a handful of games over the next nine seasons, he never managed to play a full season, his best being thirty-nine matches in 1959–60.

He only scored two goals for the club, his first coming in a 3–1 win at Sheffield United on Bonfire Day 1955 and the second in a 4–1 defeat of Charlton Athletic eight years later.

The long-serving defender left Fratton Park in July 1964 to join Aldershot, where he made seventy-eighth League appearances before hanging up his boots.

GUTHRIE, JIMMY

Born in Luncarty, near Perth in June 1912, he joined Perth Thistle and later Scone Thistle after playing for Luncarty City boys' team, where a series of outstanding performances led to him being selected for the very first Scotland v England Youth international match.

He joined Dundee, making his first team debut in 1932 and going on to play in 143 Scottish League games before signing for Portsmouth in August 1937.

His proudest moment came when he led Portsmouth to victory in the FA Cup Final of 1939 against Wolverhampton Wanderers. The outbreak of the Second World War restricted his League appearances for the Fratton Park club to seventy-six, although he made a further 213 wartime appearances for the club.

At the start of the abortive season of 1939–40, he was badly injured in a car crash and it was while he was recovering that he started to give more thought to the playing conditions of the Players Union. In 1946 he had joined Crystal Palace as player-coach but in August of that year, he was elected the fifth chairman of the Professional Footballers' Association.

H

HAINES, BILLY

William Wyndham Pretoria Haines was recommended to Portsmouth by a supporter named Fred Prescott. Manager John McCartney watched him play one game for Somerset and then offered him terms.

His first appearance for the club was for the reserves in February 1923 and he celebrated by scoring a hat-trick. Later that season, the powerfully built centre-forward had forced his way into the first team and scored on his debut in a 4–1 win over Swindon Town. The following season, Pompey won the Third Division (South) championship with Haines scoring twenty-eight goals in thirty games, including hat-tricks against Exeter City (Home 4–0) Aberdare Athletic (Home 4–0) and Norwich City (Home 4–0).

He earned his nickname of 'Farmers Boy' due to being a well-built country boy. Despite his build and power, Haines based his game and his shooting on placement rather than force and would often take penalties without a run up. He continued to score on a regular basis for Pompey and in 1926–27 when the club won promotion to the First Division, he scored forty goals in forty two games. He scored four goals against Preston North End (Home 5–1) in the final game of the season and hat-tricks against Blackpool (Home 5–0) Oldham Athletic (Home 7–2) and Clapton Orient (Away 5–4).

At Fratton Park, he scored a highly creditable 129 goals in 179 games before in May 1928 he moved to Southampton. He became as popular at the Dell as he had been at Portsmouth, scoring forty-seven goals in seventy games. He left League football in 1932 but continued to play for non-League Weymouth with enthusiasm. In 1960, he was president of Portsmouth Supporters Club.

HALIFAX TOWN

The Shaymen lost their Football League status at the end of the 1992–93 season. Having played their first Football League game on 27 August 1921 in the Third Division (North) the club enjoyed sixty-five seasons without ever winning a League Championship.

The two clubs first met in 1961–62 when a Johnny Gordon goal gave Pompey a 1–1 draw at Fratton Park and a Ron Saunders header gave the club both points in a 1–0 win at The Shay.

The sides did not meet again until 1978–79 when they were both in the Fourth Division, Portsmouth winning 3–1 at home but losing 2–0 away. The clubs last met the following season when Pompey were promoted and Halifax finished eighteenth. The Fratton Park side completed the 'double'over their Yorkshire opponents, winning 3–1 at home and 2–1 at The Shay.

HAND, EOIN

Dublin-born Eoin Hand failed to make the grade at Swindon Town and returned to Ireland to play for Dundalk and Drumcondra before Portsmouth signed him for 7,500 in October 1968.

The Republic of Ireland international made his Pompey debut in a 2–2 draw at Fulham and went on to appear in sixty-seven consecutive League games before missing his first game for the club. An ever-present in 1969–70, he went on to appear in 307 League and Cup games in two spells for the Fratton Park club.

After being given a free transfer, he joined Limerick United as player-manager and in his first season in charge, guided the League of Ireland club to their first championship in twenty years. He also took over as part-time team manager of the republic of Ireland in the summer of 1980 and stayed in charge until the arrival of Jack Charlton.

He later managed Huddersfield Town, but surprisingly lost his job with the Terriers standing fourth in the Third Division.

HARRIS, HARRY

Signed from Newport County for £10,000 in July 1958, this versatile player went on to give the club thirteen seasons great service.

He made his debut at inside-left in a 2–1 defeat at home to West Ham United on the opening day of the 1958–59 season and he played in the first thirty nine matches of the club's last campaign in the First Division, scoring thirteen goals.

His first two goals for the club came in the 2–2 draw with Chelsea at Fratton Park on 6 September 1958. In 1959–60 he scored sixteen goals to be the club's second top scorer in a season in which Pompey were almost relegated again, this time to the Third Division.

Moving to wing-half, he was an ever-present in 1964–65 and in 1966–67 only missed the final game of the season. He scored forty-nine goals in 426 League and Cup games for Pompey before returning to end his career with Newport County.

HARRIS, PETER

Winger Peter Harris made his debut for Portsmouth as an eighteen year old  against Watford in October 1944. A week later he scored two goals on his home debut in a 3–0 win over Aldershot and two more the following week as Queen's Park Rangers were beaten 4–1.

After establishing himself as a first team regular in 1947–48, he ended the following season, when the club won the Championship, as the joint top-scorer in the League with seventeen goals and in the 7–0 FA Cup win over Stockport County, hit the first of his eight senior hat-tricks.

This flying winger with an astonishing turn of speed and superb ball control won the first of his two England caps against the Republic of

Ireland in September 1949. That season, he scored sixteen goals in the League as Pompey retained the League Championship.

His best season to date for the club in terms of goals scored was 1952–53 when he top scored with twenty-three League goals, including a hat-trick in the 5–2 win over Sunderland. He netted twenty the following season including three goals in the 5–1 defeat of Liverpool. In 1954–55 he equalled his best tally with twenty-three goals, including four in the 6–2 defeat of Sheffield United. The following season he again netted twenty-three goals and in the match against Aston Villa on 3 September 1958 he scored all five goals in the 5–2 win. Unfortunately their prolific goal scorer did not prevent Pompey from finishing bottom of the First Division and being relegated.

In November 1959, after a serious chest ailment had forced him to spend a long time in a sanatorium, Peter Harris played the last of his 520 games for Pompey, in which he had scored 208 goals.

HATELEY, MARK

A prolific scorer with Coventry City's youth team and reserves, he got his first team chance at Highfield Road against Wolverhampton Wanderers in May 1979. He became a regular in 1982–83 and was the club's top scorer, earning selection for England Under-21s. On his international debut he scored twice and in the club's game at The Dell, he scored a hat-trick in a 5–5 draw.

His departure from the Sky Blues was acrimonious. Portsmouth, then in Division Two, offered just £50,000 for his services and a tribunal set the fee at £190,000 – a figure still a bargain for a player on the verge of the full England squad. Within twelve months, he won the first of his thirty-two caps and in the second game of

England's South American tour, scored against Brazil in the Maracana. Hateley only spent one season at Fratton Park, 1983–84, scoring twenty-five goals in forty-four appearances. In the space of four days in November, he scored hat-tricks against Cambridge United and Grimsby Town.

His goal against Brazil elevated him to superstar status and ten days later he was on his way to AC Milan for £1 million. After three years at the San Siro he moved to Monaco before in 1990 joining Glasgow Rangers. After 216 games for the Ibrox club he moved back south to play for Queen's Park Rangers and is now player-manager of Hull City.

HAT-TRICK HEROES

The scorer of the club's first hat-trick was Sandy Brown who hit three goals in the 10–0 FA Cup victory over Ryde on 30 September 1899. The scorer of the club's first hat-trick in the Football League was Percy Cherrett who hit three of Pompey's goals in a 4–1 win over Gillingham at Fratton Park on 15 October 1921.

In 1963–64, Ron Saunders scored two hat-tricks for Portsmouth against Leyton Orient in separate games. The first was achieved after Pompey went three goals down, the second after they had been two behind. The first match was won 6–3, the second 4–3.

One of the fastest hat-tricks in the Football League came against Exeter City on 10 February 1981, when Mick Tait scored three goals in the space of five minutes.

When Billy Haines scored forty League goals in 1926–27 he netted five hat-tricks: Blackpool (Home 5–0), Oldham Athletic (Home 7–2), Clapton Orient (Away 5–4), Notts County (Home 9–1) and Preston North End (Home 5–1). He is also Pompey's leading scorer of hat-tricks with ten, followed by Jack Weddle, Duggie Reid and Peter Harris with eight.

In the club's non-League days, Jimmy Taylor scored a double hat-trick in the 7–0 win over Chesham in a Southern League Division Two game in 1911–12. Herbert Barlow also scored a double hat-trick in Pompey's 10–2 win over Bournemouth in a Football League South game in 1940–41.

There have been nine occasions when two Portsmouth players have scored hat-tricks in the same match but none of them in the Football League. The first came on 5 March 1902 when Marshall and W Smith scored three goals apiece in a 9–1 win over Millwall. Chesham were beaten 11–0 on 2 September 1911 with Cullen scoring five and J L Jones four of the goals. Frank Stringfellow and James Armstrong netted three goals each when Portsmouth beat Queen's Park Rangers 7–1 in a London Combination game in 1916–17.

The feat was achieved three times in South Hants War League games with Danagher and Turner scoring three goals apiece in the 9–0 defeat of the Special School of Flying. Turner with five goals and Whalley with three helped Pompey beat Cowes 12–0 and William James and Frank Stringfellow scored three goals each in the 6–0 win over Brighton. On 17 May 1941, Aldershot were beaten 10–5 with Barlow and Black scoring hat-tricks and the same two forwards repeated the feat in a 7–1 win over Watford at the end of the year. Herbert Barlow and Griffiths were the last two Pompey players to score hat-tricks in the same game when Fulham were beaten 9-1 on 21 March 1942.

The last Portsmouth player to score a hat-trick was Lee Bradbury who hit three goals in Pompey's 4–2 win over Barnsley on 22 April 1997.

HEAVIEST PLAYER

Probably the heaviest player ever to play in Portsmouth's first team is goalkeeper Fred Brown. He weighed in at 14 st 11 lbs and appeared in twenty-two first team games between 1958 and 1960.

HEMMERMAN, JEFF

A forward who made his League debut for his home town club of Hull City, he had a loan spell with Scunthorpe United before joining Port Vale. Given a free transfer, he signed for Portsmouth in the summer of 1978 and made his debut in the League Cup tie against Swindon Town at the beginning of the 1978–79 season. He scored twice for Pompey in a 5–3 defeat at York City and netted a hat-trick two games later as Crewe were beaten 3–0. He ended that season as the club's top scorer with sixteen League and Cup goals.

Hemmerman scored thirteen League goals the following season as the club were promoted to Division Three. He played the last of his 138 games for the club against Millwall on the final day of the 1981–82 season before joining Cardiff City, first as a player and then as physiotherapist.

HENDERSON, JIMMY

Born in Johnshaven in Scotland, he never played soccer as a schoolboy but joined a youth club side at Kirkintilloch as a teenager. Portsmouth were quick to spot his potential and signed him in January 1949 when they were one of the most successful sides in the country. Making his debut as a centre-forward in a 3–1 defeat at Sunderland in September 1951, he soon established himself as a first team regular.

He won the first of seven Scottish caps against Sweden in May 1953 and his last against Northern Ireland in 1959. After 233 League and Cup appearances for Pompey, in which he scored seventy-three goals, he moved to Wolverhampton Wanderers in March 1958 but only stayed eight months before he was on the move again. When he signed for Arsenal, the Scot captured some of his old form, playing on the wing as he had done for most of his time at Fratton Park. He joined Fulham in January 1962 but unfortunately for the Cottagers he proved to be past his best. His last move was to Poole Town in the summer of 1964.

HILAIRE, VINCE

A skilful winger, Vince Hilaire made his Football League debut for Crystal Palace, coming on as a substitute at Lincoln City in March 1977. He was a great favourite with the Selhurst Park fans and won both England Youth and Under-23 caps. Having helped the Eagles to win the Second Division championship in 1978–79, he later became unsettled and joined Luton Town in exchange for Trevor Aylott plus £100,000.

He failed to settle at Kenilworth Road and in November 1984 he joined Portsmouth. He made his debut in a 2–2 draw at home to Blackburn Rovers, scoring Pompey's second goal. A goalmaker rather than a goalscorer, he found the net twenty-five times in his 168 League and Cup games for the Fratton Park club before leaving to play for Leeds United. He later had spells with Stoke City and Exeter City before hanging up his boots.

HIRON, RAY

His early football was spent playing in the Gosport League until Fareham persuaded him to play in the Hampshire League. He had just completed his Dockyard apprenticeship as a fitter/turner when he caught Pompey's eye. Asked if he could find time during his lunch hour to have a chat with Portsmouth boss George Smith, he hitched a lift on a friend's motor bike and left a short time later to hand in his notice at the dockyard.

Five months later, he made his first team debut in a 1–1 draw at Bury. It was the start of eleven seasons at Fratton Park in which he became one of only five players in Pompey's postwar history to score 100 League goals. His first came later in that 1964–65 season in a 1–1 draw at home to Leyton Orient. In 1968–69 he top scored with seventeen goals, including four in a 5–2 win over Norwich City.

The following season he was again top scorer, this time with eighteen goals, netting a hat-trick in the final game of the season, a 3–3 draw at Hull City. He top-scored in the next two seasons, but following the arrival of Ian St John, he was allowed to leave Fratton Park. He had scored 117 League and Cup goals in 364 appearances. He then went on to play three seasons for Reading, the last as a defender.

HOGG, GRAEME

Born in Aberdeen, Graeme Hogg joined Manchester United as an apprentice. He had a disastrous start to his career with the Old Trafford club, making his debut in the Reds' 2–0 FA Cup defeat against Bournemouth in January 1984.

However, he was not discarded and went on to play in 101 League and Cup games for United before Alex Ferguson sold him to Portsmouth for £150,000 in the summer of 1988. Hogg, who made his debut in a 2–1 win at Shrewsbury Town, proved a difficult man to pass. His strengths lay in his heading and tackling and his ability to marshal the Pompey defence.

The central defender had appeared in 108 League and Cup games for the Fratton Park club when he was sold to Hearts for £200,000 in August 1991. After just over three seasons at Tynecastle, he returned to the Football League with Notts County.

HOME MATCHES

Portsmouth's best home win in the Football League is the 9–1 defeat of Notts County in a Second Division game at Fratton Park on 9 April 1927.

Pompey have scored seven goals in a League game at home on four occasions: Queen's Park Rangers 7–0 (1923–24), Oldham Athletic 7–2 (1926–27), Burnley 7–1 (1929–30) and Everton 7–0 (1949–50).

Other than Football League matches, Portsmouth's biggest home wins have been: Clapton Orient 16–1 (London War League 1941–42), Cowes 12–0 (South Hants War League 1917–18), Chesham 11–0 (Southern League Division Two 1911–12) and Royal Engineers 11–0 (Friendly 1918–19).

HOME SEASONS

Portsmouth have gone through a complete League season with an undefeated home record on just one occasion – in 1948–49 when they won eighteen and drew three of their home matches in winning the First Division championship. The club's highest number of home wins in a League season is the eighteen achieved in that season of 1948–49.

HONOURS

The club have won the following major honours:

Division One Championship	1948–49	1949–50
Division Three (South) Championship	1923–24	
Division Three Championship	1961–62	1982–83
FA Cup Winners	1939	
FA Cup Runners–Up	1929	1934
FA Charity Shield (Shared)	1949	

INJURIES

The risk of serious injury is an ever-present threat in the game of football and all professional players expect to miss games through injury at some point in their careers.

On 6 January 1906, goalkeeper George Harris, who was replacing Fred

Cook for the match at Queen's Park Rangers which Pompey lost 2–0, made one of the most dramatic recoveries following injury. He was kicked over the eye when making a brave save and then crashed into a goalpost. He was carried to the dressing room, where at one stage doctors thought he might die, yet by the end of the match the former Grimsby 'keeper was up and about.

INTERNATIONAL MATCHES

Fratton Park was the venue for the England v Wales international match on 2 March 1903 which the home side won 2–1 with goals from Joe Bache (Aston Villa) and Viv Woodward (Tottenham Hotspur). The only Portsmouth player to appear for England was Albert Houlker.

In March 1938, France were on the look out for opposition after their planned international against Austria had been postponed following Hitler's annexation of that country. It looked for some time that Portsmouth would be travelling to Paris to fulfil the fixture, but in the end, Belgium provided the opposition.

INTERNATIONAL PLAYERS

Portsmouth's most capped player (ie: caps gained while players were registered with the club) is Jimmy Dickinson with forty-eight caps. Here is a complete list of players who have gained full international honours while at Fratton Park:

England		J G Henderson	5	Wales	
J Allen	2	J Scoular	9	F Cook	6
D Cunliffe	1	A Wilson	1	R T Davies	1
J Dickinson	48	**Northern Ireland**		B Horne	8
J Froggatt	13	T Casey	2	G T Maguire	7
P Harris	2	C Clarke	13	P S Roberts	4
M Hateley	4	H Davey	1	C J Symons	18
A Houlker	2	D Dougan	1	**Republic of Ireland**	
A E Knight	1	D Hanna	1	E K Hand	20
L Phillips	3	R Irvine	2	M J Kelly	4
J Smith	3	J McAlinden	4	J McAlinden	2
F Worrall	2	J A Mackie	2	A McLoughlin	19
Scotland		M Reilly	2	K O'Callaghan	4
J Easson	3	N Uprichard	13		

Pompey's first player to be capped was D R Hanna who played for Northern Ireland v Wales in 1899.

J

JACKSON, BOB

As a player, Bob Jackson scored over 400 goals in non-League soccer before joining Tranmere Rovers at the age of twenty-eight. Unfortunately his career was ended shortly afterwards by injury and after a spell as coach with Bolton Wanderers and as manager of Southern League Worcester City, he joined Pompey as chief scout. Following Jack Tinn's retirement, Jackson was appointed manager and made Ike Clarke, a powerfully-built centre-forward from West Bromwich Albion, his first major signing.

After finishing eighth in 1947–48, his first season in charge, he steered Pompey to two successive League championships. In 1948–49 they ended the season five points clear of Manchester United and in 1949–50 they pipped Wolverhampton Wanderers on goal average.

It was something of a surprise when Jackson left Fratton Park for Hull City in 1952, after being offered a five year contract, for Portsmouth were still challenging for honours. Bolton-born Jackson had a number of running battles with the Board at Boothferry Park and after three years of struggling, he was sacked. He sued the club for breach of contract and left the game very disillusioned.

JENNINGS, NICK

Born in Wellington, Somerset, Nick Jennings played his early football with his home town club before signing for Plymouth Argyle in the summer of 1963. He made ninety-eight League appearances for the Home Park club before joining Portsmouth in January 1967.

He made his debut for the Fratton Park club on his twenty-first birthday, scoring one of the goals in a 3–2 win over Rotherham United. The following season he scored his first hat-trick for the club in a 3–1 win at Norwich City.

The tricky outside-left went on to play for Pompey for eight seasons, scoring fifty-one goals in 227 first team appearances. He left Fratton Park at the end of the 1973–74 season to join Exeter City after a short loan spell at Aldershot.

K

KAMARA, CHRIS

An aggressive all-action midfield ball winner who turned out to be an instant hit wherever he played. He had a habit of returning to clubs as his career unfolded.

Chris Kamara joined Pompey from the Royal Navy and made his debut against Luton Town in September 1975, scoring his first goal on his third full appearance in a 4–1 defeat at Bolton Wanderers.

Surprisingly on the eve of the 1977–78 season, he was allowed to join Swindon Town for £17,000.

He had played in 147 League games for the County Ground club when in the summer of 1981, he returned to Fratton Park. He only played in eleven League games in his second spell with the club and after just two months joined Brentford. He scored twenty eight goals in 152 League appearances for the Griffin Park outfit before returning to Swindon Town. There followed spells at Stoke, Leeds, Luton and Sheffield United before he joined Bradford City as manager.

KELLARD, BOBBY

Small, stocky ball-winning wing-half Bobby Kellard served eight different League clubs and had two spells with Portsmouth.

An England Youth international, he made 106 appearances for Southend United before joining Crystal Palace in September 1963. Two years later he joined Ipswich Town before in March 1966 he signed for Pompey.

He made his debut for the Fratton Park club in a 1–0 defeat at home to Birmingham City but after that the club only lost two of its last ten matches to finish in mid-table. After playing in 102 games, he was transferred to Bristol City. A spell at Leicester City followed before he rejoined Crystal Palace in September 1971.

Fifteen months later, he returned to Fratton Park for a second spell, appearing in a further seventy four first team games before ending his career with spells at Hereford United and Torquay United.

KIRBY, BILL

Signed from Swindon Town in 1905, centre-forward Bill Kirby made his Pompey debut in a Western League match at home to Queen's Park Rangers on 15 March 1905. The following season he scored his first hat-trick for the club in a 5–1 win over Bristol Rovers. In 1906–07, he top scored in the Southern League with twenty-one goals, netting another hat-trick in the 6–0 defeat of Crystal Palace.

At the end of that season, the club embarked on a tour of Germany and Austria and in the first match against Leipzig, Kirby scored four goals in a 6–1 win. He continued to score on a regular basis and in October 1910, he was granted a benefit after scoring his 100th goal for the club – the match producing £200 for the centre-forward.

In 1911, after scoring 117 goals in 305 games, the Preston-born forward returned to his home town to play for Preston North End. He played in fifty five League games for the Deepdale club, scoring twenty-two goals.

KNIGHT, ALAN

The longest serving player at Fratton Park, Alan Knight made his Pompey debut at the age of sixteen in a 1–0 win at Rotherham United on the final day of the 1977–78 season.

An England Youth and Under-21 international, Knight became the club's regular 'keeper in 1981–82. He was an ever-present the following season when the club won the Third Division championship and again for the next two seasons, playing in 158 consecutive League games. The Balham-born goalkeeper was also an ever-present during the club's promotion-winning season in Division Two in 1986–87, keeping twenty clean sheets in the forty-two match programme.

Alan Knight, an excellent shotstopper, passed Peter Bonetti's League record of goalkeeping appearances for one club during the 1995–96 season. At the time of writing he has played in 751 first team games for the Fratton Park club, 642 of them in the Football League.

KNIGHT, ARTHUR

Arthur Egerton Knight became something of a legendary character during his thirteen years on Pompey's books. An amateur from Godalming, he joined the Fratton Park club in 1908 and made his first team debut in a 4–3 win at Croydon Common in November 1909.

The following month, Knight made his debut at left-back for the England amateur international side in a 9–1 win over Holland.

He played thirty one times for the England amateur side and made his only appearance for the full England side against Northern Ireland in October 1919, although he played against Wales in a 'Victory' match later that month.

In 1912, Knight was selected for the Stockholm Olympic Games squad. Playing in all three games, he won a gold medal as the United Kingdom beat Denmark 4–2 in the final.

In November 1912 he outstanding performances in the colours of Portsmouth was marked, when he was presented with a silver mounted walking stick at a club dinner.

Pompey's first season of League football was Knight's final season with the club. He had played in 183 games for the Fratton Park side before leaving in 1921 to play for Corinthians.

KUHL, MARTIN

After joining Birmingham City as an apprentice, he went on to appear in 132 first team games for the St Andrews Club before moving to Sheffield United in March 1987. A year later, he had left the Blades to play for Watford. Unable to settle at Vicarage Road he signed for Portsmouth in September 1988 and made his debut in a 2–1 defeat at Bradford City.

Although not a prolific scorer from midfield, he was joint top scorer with Colin Clarke in 1990–91 with thirteen goals. Reverting to more of a defensive midfield role, he began to impress other clubs and after appearing in 181 games for the Fratton Park club in which he scored twenty-eight goals, he joined Derby County for £650,000 in September 1992.

He played in eighty games for the Rams before a short loan spell with Notts County. He later signed for Bristol City for £300,000 and soon settled down to demonstrate his capabilities and in his first full season with the club was voted 'Player of the Year'.

L

LATE FINISHES

Portsmouth's final match of the season against Derby County at Fratton Park on 31 May 1947 is the latest date for the finish of any Pompey season. During the war, many curious things occurred, among them the continuance of the 1939–40 season into June. Portsmouth's last competitive match in that campaign was on 8 June when two goals from Wilkinson gave them a 2–2 draw at Reading.

LEADING GOAL SCORERS

Portsmouth have provided the Football League's divisional leading goalscorer on three occasions. They are:

1963–64	Ron Saunders	Division Two	33 goals
1986–87	Mick Quinn	Division Two	22 goals
1992–93	Guy Whittingham	Division One	42 goals

In 1979–80, Colin Garwood was the Fourth Division's leading goalscorer with twenty-seven goals, seventeen of which he scored with Portsmouth.

LEAGUE GOALS: CAREER HIGHEST

Peter Harris holds the Portsmouth record for the most League goals with a career total of 193 goals scored between 1946 and 1960.

LEAGUE GOALS: LEAST CONCEDED

During the 1986–87 season, Portsmouth conceded just twenty-eight goals in forty-two games when finishing runners up to Derby County in the race for the Second Division championship.

LEAGUE GOALS: MOST CONCEDED

Portsmouth conceded 112 League goals during 1958–59 when they finished bottom of the First Division and were relegated.

LEAGUE GOALS: MOST INDIVIDUAL

Guy Whittingham holds the Portsmouth record for the most League goals in a season with forty-two scored in the First Division during the 1992–93 season.

LEAGUE GOALS: MOST SCORED

Portsmouth's highest goal tally in the Football League was during the 1979–80 season when they scored ninety-one goals in finishing fourth in Division Four to win promotion.

LEAGUE VICTORY: HIGHEST

Portsmouth's best League victory was the 9–1 win over Notts County at Fratton Park on 9 April 1927. Billy Haines scored a hat-trick, Jerry Mackie and Fred Cook two goals apiece and Reg Davies and Fred Forward also got one the scoresheet.

LEVER, EDDIE

Eddie Lever arrived at Fratton Park in 1929 and though he never played in Portsmouth's first team, he always retained some links with the club although he had been released and was teaching in nearby Alton.

He was appointed reserve team coach in the late 1940s and in August 1952, he replaced Bob Jackson as Pompey manager after he had accepted a lucrative offer to manage Hull City.

Having discovered Jimmy Dickinson whilst teaching, the first thing he did was to make him captain. His first move in the transfer market was to sign goalkeeper Norman Uprichard from Swindon. The Northern Ireland international was later followed by Derek Dougan from Distillery, who went on to play for Northern Ireland on forty-three occasions. The club were often struggling near the foot of the First Division when Lever was in charge, but in 1954–55 they finished third, just four points behind champions Chelsea. In 1957–58, Pompey narrowly avoided relegation and after a link of almost thirty years, Lever parted company with the club.

LONDON WAR CUP FINAL

In 1942, Portsmouth reached the final of the London War Cup at Wembley, only to lose 2–0 to Brentford in front of a 72,000 crowd. Pompey finished first in their group after the following results to qualify for the semi-final.

	Home	Away
Fulham	9–1	1–2
Crystal Palace	2–1	2–0
Chelsea	2–0	0–0

A crowd of 19,036 saw an Andy Black goal good enough to beat Charlton Athletic 1–0 in the semi-final played at Stamford Bridge.

Pompey's team in the final was: Walker; Rookes; Rochford; Guthrie Flewin; Wharton; Bullock; Griffiths; Black; Barlow and Parker.

LONG SERVICE

Jimmy Dickinson joined Pompey in January 1944 and played his last game for the club in April 1965. After working at Fratton Park as a public relations officer and Club Secretary, he was appointed manager in 1977.

He resigned that position in August 1979 after suffering a heart attack, to become the club's chief executive. Sadly, the legendary Dickinson died in November 1982 after almost thirty-nine years loyal service to the Fratton Park club.

Longest serving manager is Jack Tinn who was in charge of the club for twenty years from 1927 to 1947.

Among Pompey's longest serving players are Alan Knight (1977–1997) Alex Wilson (1951–1966) Reg Flewin (1938–1953) Peter Harris (1946–1959) and John Milkins (1960–1973).

LOWEST

The lowest number of goals cored by Portsmouth in a single Football League season is thirty-two in 1975–76 when the club finished bottom of the Second Division and were relegated.

The club's lowest points record in the Football League occurred in 1958–59 when Pompey gained just twenty-one points and were relegated from the First Division.

McCANN, ALBERT

Playing his early football for Luton Town and Coventry City, Albie McCann joined Portsmouth from the Highfield Road club for £6,000 in the summer of 1962.

He made his debut in a 1–0 win over Derby County and played in all thirty-eight games that remained that season. The Maidenhead-born inside-forward was the club's leading scorer in 1965–66 and 1967–68 and was joint top-scorer in 1966–67 when he scored his first hat-trick for the club in a 3–3 draw at Bristol City.

He gave great service but towards the end of the 1973–74 season, after scoring ninety-eight goals in 379 games, he left Fratton Park for a new career in South Africa.

McCARTNEY, JOHN

A player with Newton Heath, the forerunners of Manchester United, he began his managerial career at Barnsley, where he had complete control of team affairs, which was rather unusual at this time. Despite improving the club's financial position, he sold Benny Green to Birmingham City and the team's form slumped dramatically.

The Glasgow-born McCartney returned north of the border to manage St Mirren and took them to the Scottish Cup Final and runners-up in the First Division on two occasions. He then managed Heart of Midlothian for ten years before moving south to take charge at Portsmouth in 1920.

He gradually developed what was to become known as the 'Pompey Style' and in 1923–24 the club lifted the Third Division (South) title.

Three years later Pompey were in the First Division but in May 1927 McCartney had to resign because of ill health. However, four months later, he took over at Luton Town where he had played but again he was dogged by ill health and this finally forced his resignation and his retirement from football.

There was plenty of affection for this hard working manager and the launching of a testimonial fund quickly realised £300. In January 1933 John McCartney died and was buried just a short distance from the Heart of Midlothian ground where both he and his brother, Willie, had been successful managers.

McLOUGHLIN, ALAN

A former Manchester United apprentice, he failed to make the first team at Old Trafford and so moved to Swindon Town on a free transfer. He played in just nine League games for the Robins before being loaned out to Torquay United. However, he returned to the County Ground to become one of Swindon's most influential players. After scoring Swindon's goal which defeated Sunderland in the 1990 Wembley play-offs, he was immediately signed by Southampton for £1 million.

At the Dell, McLoughlin was never played in his favourite position – just behind the front two – and soon lost his place. He had a one match loan spell at Aston Villa but in February 1992, he joined Portsmouth for £400,000.

This Republic of Ireland international, winner of twenty eight caps, made his Pompey debut in a goalless draw at Wolverhampton Wanderers. Since then he has appeared in 244 League and Cup games for the Fratton Park club, playing in two FA Cup semi-finals as well as a couple of play-off semi-finals.

MACKIE, ALEX

Irish international full-back Alex Mackie was signed from Arsenal in the summer of 1928 and made his Pompey debut on 27 October in a 4–1 home win over Bury. He appeared in thirty-one games that season and in the same number in 1929–30. The Belfast-born defender was an ever-present in 1930–31 when the club finished fourth in the First Division and again the following season, establishing a run of 136 consecutive League appearances.

He was capped twice for Northern Ireland during his stay at Fratton Park, against Scotland in 1934 and Wales in 1935, and picked up an FA Cup losers' medal against Manchester City in 1934.

He played the last of his 286 games for the club in April 1935 in a 1–0 defeat at home to Wolverhampton Wanderers and a year later, he joined Northampton Town.

MACKIE, JERRY

Motherwell-born Jerry Mackie joined Portsmouth from Blantyre Celtic in 1920 and made his debut in October of that year at Millwall in what was Pompey's first season in the Football League. In 1922–23 he was the club's top scorer with ten goals and in the following season he scored twelve and created many for top scorer Billy Haines as Pompey won the Third Division (South) championship. He was equal top-scorer in 1924–25 with seventeen goals as Pompey finished fourth in the Second Division, hitting a hat-trick in a 5–0 win over Bradford City in the final game of the season.

He was a most popular player in his eight seasons at Fratton Park and scored eighty-two goals in his 263 League and Cup appearances before signing for Southampton in March 1928.

Mackie had the great satisfaction of scoring a hat-trick on his home debut against Barnsley. He was a shrewd Scottish schemer and he forged a successful partnership for the Saints with Billy Haines, just as he had at Portsmouth.

MANAGERS

Since it was formed in 1898 to the time of writing Portsmouth FC has had twenty-three managers. Longest in the job was Jack Tinn. He covered twenty years, from 1927–1947. Second longest-serving was Bob Brown with ten years and John McCartney comes a close third with seven years in the 1920s.

This is the complete list of Portsmouth's managers with the inclusive dates in which they held office:

1898–1901	Frank Brettell	1973–1974	John Mortimore
1901–1904	Robert Blyth	1974	Ron Tindall
1904–1908	Richard Bonney	1974–1977	Ian St John
1911–1920	Bob Brown	1977–1979	Jimmy Dickinson
1920–1927	John McCartney	1979–1982	Frank Burrows
1927–1947	Jack Tinn	1982–1984	Bobby Campbell
1947–1952	Bob Jackson	1984–1989	Alan Ball
1952–1958	Eddie Lever	1989–1990	John Gregory
1958–1961	Freddie Cox	1990–1991	Frank Burrows
1961	Bill Thompson	1991–1995	Jim Smith
1961–1970	George Smith	1995–	Terry Fenwick
1970–1973	Ron Tindall		

MARATHON MATCHES

Pompey have been involved in a number of cup games that have gone to three matches. These were: Blackburn Rovers (FA Cup second round 1924–25); Derby County (FA Cup third round 1925–26); Scunthorpe United (FA Cup fourth round 1953–54); Coventry City (FA Cup fourth round 1962–63); Hull City (FA Cup third round 1966–67); Orient (FA Cup fourth round 1973–74); Wimbledon (FA Cup second round 1979–80) and Tottenham Hotspur (League Cup fourth round 1985–86).

MARINELLO, PETER

As a teenager with Hibernian, Peter Marinello's wing play had brought him the tag of the 'Second George Best'. He had made his League debut in Scotland as a seventeen year old and was only nineteen when Arsenal brought him south for £100,000. He played in tirty eight League games for the Gunners before joining Portsmouth in July 1973.

He made his debut for the Fratton Park club in a 1–0 defeat at Middlesbrough on the opening day of the 1973–74 season and in his first two seasons with the club played in thirty-nine games in each campaign.

He went on to play in 110 League and Cup games, scoring ten goals before he left to play for Motherwell in December 1975 for around a quarter of the fee he had cost.

MARKSMEN: LEAGUE

Portsmouth's top League goalscorer is Peter Harris, who struck 193 League goals during his fifteen years at Fratton Park. Only eight players have hit more than 100 League goals for the club.

1	Peter Harris	193		6	Ray Hiron	110
2	Jack Weddle	170		7	Johnny Gordon	105
3	Ron Saunders	140		8	Jimmy Easson	102
4	Duggie Reid	129		9	Guy Whittingham	88
5	Billy Haines	119		10	Albert McCann	84

MARKSMEN: OVERALL

Nine players have hit a century of goals for Portsmouth. The club's top marksman is Peter Harris. The Century Club consists of:

1	Peter Harris	208		6	Ray Hiron	117
2	Jack Weddle	183		7	Johnny Gordon	116
3	Ron Saunders	157		8	Jimmy Easson	107
4	Duggie Reid	134		9	Guy Whittingham	101
5	Billy Haines	128				

MARTIN, JIMMY

Portsmouth signed left-half Jimmy Martin from Hearts after he had played his early football with Glasgow Rangers.

He arrived at Fratton Park in November 1920 and made his debut the following month in a 1–0 win over Watford. A regular over the next six seasons, he only missed the last match of the 1923–24 season as Pompey won the Third Division championship. He went on to play in 225 League and Cup games scoring twenty-nine goals before leaving to join Aldershot.

He shared a benefit with David Watson, the club's other Scottish inside-forward when 6,000 saw Pompey draw 1–1 with Hearts, the first Scottish side to visit Fratton Park.

MELLOR, PETER

Goalkeeper Peter Mellor joined Manchester City as an apprentice from school but having failed to make the grade, he joined Witton Albion. However, in April 1969, Burnley stepped in with a £1,750 bid and he joined the Turf Moor club. Yet despite being an ever-present in his first season with the Clarets, he was barracked and joined Fulham.

At Craven Cottage he missed very few games and was outstanding in the club's run to Wembley in 1975. He later had one season with Hereford United after falling out with Fulham boss, Bobby Campbell, before joining Portsmouth.

Making his debut at home to Bradford City on the opening day of the 1978–79 season, he went on to appear in every game that season, keeping nineteen clean sheets plus another two in Cup competitions. The following season he made a number of important saves as Pompey won promotion to the Third Division. He retired after playing the last of his 146 League and Cup games in May 1981.

MERTHYR TOWN

Founder members of the Third Division in 1920. They then spent the next nine seasons in the Third Division (South) before losing their place at the end of the 1929–30 season.

The two clubs first met at Fratton Park on 11 December 1920 when the game was goalless. The return the following February saw Merthyr win 2–1. In 1921–22 both sides won their home fixture 2–1 and the following season the game at Fratton Park was a 1–1 draw and Merthyr continued their good home form beating Pompey 3–0. The clubs last met in 1923–24 when Portsmouth won the Third Division (South) championship. They secured their first point at Merthyr in a 2–2 draw and then won the home fixture 1–0 with Billy Haines the scorer.

MILKINS, JOHN

Goalkeeper John Milkins joined Pompey straight from school and after gaining England Youth international honours, made his debut on 5 November 1960 against Leyton Orient.

Despite turning professional at the end of that season he faced stiff competition from John Armstrong and Dick Beattie and did not become a regular in the first team until early 1965.

In the next nine years, Milkins missed very few games and was an ever-present in 1968–69. An excellent handler of the ball, even in the most difficult of conditions, he played in 389 League and Cup games for Portsmouth before losing his place to David Best and joined Oxford United for £10,000.

He played in fifty-nine first team games for the Manor Ground club before being released at the end of the 1979–80 season.

MORTIMORE, JOHN

A commanding centre-half with Chelsea, John Mortimore made 279 appearances for the Stamford Bridge club and was an ever-present when the Blues won promotion to the First Division in 1962–63.

He was managing in Greece when he was asked to take over as Pompey boss from his former Chelsea colleague Ron Tindall. He spent heavily on the transfer market, paying £155,000 for Fulham defender Paul Went. Yet there was a financial crisis at Fratton Park and he had to make eleven of the playing staff available for transfer to offset the club's debts.

In September 1974 he was sacked and after a spell as Lawrie McMenemy's assistant at Southampton, he worked abroad, taking Benfica to the Portuguese League and Cup double.

MOST MATCHES

Portsmouth played their most number of matches, 61 in 1993–94 season. This comprised 46 League games, two FA Cup games, seven Football League Cup games and six Anglo-Italian Cup games.

N

NEILL, WARREN

Full-back Warren Neill won England Schoolboy honours before joining Queen's Park Rangers in 1980. The Acton-born defender went on to appear in 181 League games for the Loftus Road club before joining Portsmouth in the summer of 1988.

He made his debut in a 2–1 win at Shrewsbury Town on the opening day of the 1988–89 season and though he was continually hampered by injuries during his seven seasons at Fratton Park, he played in 252 League and Cup games for the club. His injuries eventually caught up with him and at the end of the 1995–96 season, he retired with a back injury. However, having played a few non-contract games for Watford, he found himself plunged into the Vicarage Road club's first team during an injury crisis.

NEUTRAL GROUNDS

When Fratton Park has been used as a neutral ground for FA Cup matches Pompey themselves have had to replay on a neutral ground a number of times:

Date	Opponents	Venue	FA Cup	Score
09.02.1925	Blackburn Rovers	Highbury	Rd 2	0–1
18.01.1926	Derby County	Filbert St	Rd 3	0–2
08.02.1954	Scunthorpe Utd	Highbury	Rd 4	4–0
19.03.1963	Coventry City	White Hart Ln	Rd 4	1–2
06.02.1967	Hull City	Highfield Rd	Rd 3	3–1
05.02.1974	Orient	Selhurst Park	Rd 4	2–0

The club's FA Cup semi-finals were, of course, played on neutral grounds. Of their appearances in this stage of the competition, four have been at Highbury and one at St Andrews. The Liverpool replay in 1991–92 was at Villa Park.

Pompey also played Wolverhampton Wanderers for the Charity Shield at Highbury and their appearances at Wembley in the FA Cup Final also qualify for inclusion.

NEWPORT COUNTY

Newport County played more matches than any other ex-member of the Football League. In the sixty-one seasons after they joined the newly formed Third Division in 1920, they played 2,672 games.

Champions of the Third Division (South) in 1938–39, they spent just one season in the Second Division. The only other time they won promotion was from the Fourth Division in 1979–80. They lost their League place automatically after finishing bottom of the Fourth Division in 1987–88.

The two clubs first met in that 1920–21 season when Newport did the double over Pompey, winning 2–0 at Fratton Park and 1–0 at home. The following season, Pompey won 4–3 at home in a seven–goal thriller and played out a goal-less draw at Somerton Park. On 29 August 1923, Pompey beat the Welsh side 5–0 at home with Watson and Haines both scoring two goals as they went on to win the Third Division (South) championship.

After that season there was a gap of thirty eight years before the two clubs met again, but when they did Pompey again won 5–0, this time at Somerton Park. In 1979–80 Newport again did the double over Pompey as both clubs won promotion from the Fourth Division but Portsmouth gained revenge when the two clubs met in the first round of the FA Cup, winning 1–0.

The last time the clubs met was 16 April 1983 when Pompey triumphed 3–0 at Somerton Park with Billy Rafferty scoring two of the goals and Alan Biley the other.

NICHOL, JIMMY

Glasgow-born right-half Jimmy Nichol made his name with Gillingham before signing for Portsmouth in November 1927. He made his League debut for Pompey in a 2–2 draw against Birmingham City at Fratton Park, five days after putting pen to paper.

For the next eight seasons, he was a regular in the Pompey side, missing very few matches and was ever-present in 1933–34. That season Nichol picked up his second FA Cup losers' medal as Pompey lost 2–1 to Manchester City, having been a member of the 1929 side that lost to Bolton Wanderers. He helped to establish the club as a First Division force, paving the way to Pompey's successive League Championships shortly after the Second World War.

He had played in 383 League and Cup games for Portsmouth, scoring nine goals, when in May 1937 he left Fratton Park to return to Gillingham.

NICKNAMES

Portsmouth Football Club are known as Pompey after the name of The Pompey public house that stands immediately outside the main entrance to the club's ground in Frogmore Road.

A number of the club's players in the pre-Football League days were known by their nickname. These included George 'Bogey' Harris, John 'Sailor' Hunter, Matthew 'Ginger' Reilly, William 'Sunny Jim' Kirby and Edward Turner who was known as 'Old Hookey'.

NON-LEAGUE

Since joining the Football League in 1920–21, Portsmouth have played non-League opposition in the FA Cup on a number of occasions. The results have been as follows:

Date	Opponents	Venue	Stage	Score
01.12.1923	London Caledonians	Away	1st Rd	5–0
15.01.1972	Boston United	Away	3rd Rd	1–0
11.12.1976	Minehead	Home	2nd Rd	2–1
26.11.1977	Bideford	Home	1st Rd	3–1

NUMBERED SHIRTS

When Portsmouth played Huddersfield Town at Highbury on 25 March 1939 in the FA Cup semi-final, it was the first time shirts had been numbered for a club match. It was a lucky omen for Pompey, who came from behind to win 2–1 and reach their third FA Cup Final.

The numbering of players shirts in the Football League became official at the start of the 1939–40 season and on 26 August 1939 Pompey wore numbered shirts in a League match for the first time when they beat Blackburn Rovers at Fratton Park 2–1 with goals from Anderson and Worrall.

O

OLDEST PLAYER

The oldest player to line-up in a Portsmouth team is Jimmy Dickinson. He was exactly forty years old when he played his last game for the club against Northampton Town (Away 1–1) on 24 April 1965.

OVERSEAS PLAYERS

The first overseas player to pull on a Pompey jersey was Swedish international Dan Ekner who played just four times for the Fratton Park club after making his debut in a 2–2 draw at home to Sunderland in November 1949. Also Belgian-born Marcel Gaillard played in sixty-fourLeague and Cup games between 1950 and 1952.

Ivan Golac, Southampton's Yugoslavian international full-back appeared in eight games for Pompey while on loan during the 1984–85 season.

Danish striker Tommy Christensen played in just three League games for Portsmouth as a non-contract player in 1985–86, scoring in two of them. His fellow countryman Bjorn Kristensen arrived from Newcastle United in 1993 and went on to appear in ninety first team games.

Dutch striker Jeroen Boere joined Portsmouth on loan in March 1994 and though he was strong in the air, he failed to score in any of his five appearances.

Predrag Radosavljevic better known as Preki, joined Pompey from Everton in the summer of 1994. The Yugoslavian scored seven goals in forty-five League and Cup games before going to play in America. Other players with foreign-sounding surnames include Sammy Igoe, Albert Juliussen, Chris Kamara, Peter Marinello and John Ruggiero – all of them born in the British Isles.

OWN GOALS

Although there have been a number of instances of own goals over the years perhaps the one by Pompey's Reg Flewin on 5 January 1946 has had the most effect.

FA Cup holders Portsmouth played their first match in defence of the trophy at St Andrews, losing 1–0 to Birmingham City courtesy of Flewin's tragic mistake and as the second game at Fratton Park four days later was goal-less, the club's hold on the trophy was broken.

P

PARKER, CLIFF

Signed from Doncaster Rovers in December 1933, Cliff Parker stayed with the club until the early 1950s. A powerful winger, he gave great service, scoring two of Pompey's goals in the 4–1 FA Cup Final win over Wolverhampton Wanderers in 1939.

He was an ever-present in 1936–37 when the club finished ninth in the First Division and topped the scoring charts with twelve goals. An ever-present again the following season, he scored fifteen League goals, including a hat-trick against Brentford in a 4–1 win, finishing second in the scoring charts to Jimmy Beattie. Parker played in every match in 1938–39 and had appeared in 126 consecutive League games when the Second World War broke out.

He was still the club's first-choice left-winger when football resumed after the hostilities.

A skilful and determined player, he was one of the most accurate passers of a ball in the game. He played in five games during the club's first Championship success in 1948–49 and three the following season as the club retained the title. He played the last of his 257 League and Cup games for Pompey in which he scored sixty-four goals in April 1951 at the age of thirty seven.

PENALTIES

One of Pompey's best penalty-takers was Cliff Parker, who had the ability to strike a ball accurately. During a wartime match against Clapton Orient, Portsmouth were awarded a penalty and as Parker placed the ball on the spot, he indicated to the Orient 'keeper that he would hit the ball to his right. He then stepped back and on the referee's whistle, stroked the ball along the ground to the 'keeper's right. The Orient custodian had gone to his left and Cliff with a wide grin on his face said to the 'keeper: 'I told you so, didn't I?'

When Pompey played Notts County at Fratton Park on 22 September 1973, the visitors missed three attempts at a spot-kick. Kevin Randall's kick was ordered to be retaken because the goalkeeper moved. Don Masson's effort was ruled out because the referee had not signalled for him to take the kick and then Brian Stubbs failed with the third. Yet despite these misses, County still won 2–1.

During the club's Third Division championship winning season of 1982–83, Pompey missed nine penalty kicks. Six different players were involved before newly signed Kevin Dillon missed two against Reading on Easter Saturday.

PHILLIPS, LEN

After playing his early football with Hackney Boys, he was called up into the Royal Marines and served on assault landing craft and took part in the Normandy D-Day landing.

Discovered playing for the Royal Marines he signed for Portsmouth in

February 1946, making his first appearance for his new club later that month against Wolverhampton Wanderers.

He made his League debut for the Portsmouth in a 1–0 win at Blackburn Rovers on 28 December 1946. However he did not establish himself in the first team until 1948–49 when Pompey won the League Championship for the first time. After that he missed just one game and scored eleven goals.

Phillips formed a terrific partnership with winger Peter Harris and helped the club to a second successive League Championship in 1949–50. The following season he won the first of three England caps when he played against Northern Ireland at Villa Park. He was never on the losing side when he represented his country and was unfortunate not to win many more caps.

After tearing a ligament in an FA Cup tie at Grimsby Town in January 1956 he was forced to leave the League scene after scoring fifty goals in 270 first team games, though he later played non-League football for Poole Town, Chelmsford and Bath City.

PIPER, NORMAN

Norman Piper began his Football League career with Plymouth Argyle, making his debut at Ipswich Town in January 1964. Over the next five seasons, he was virtually an automatic choice, playing in whatever position best suited the team.

From Youth international, he was selected for overseas summer tours with the FA and then won four caps for England at Under-23 level. After making 233 League and Cup appearances for the Home Park club he joined Portsmouth in a 40,000 deal and made his debut at Norwich City on the opening day of the 1970–71 season, scoring Pompey's goal in a 1–1 draw.

An ever-present in his first two seasons at Fratton Park, he played in 101 consecutive League games from making his debut. Although not a prolific scorer, he went on to net fifty-seven goals in 355 first team appearances during his seven years at Fratton Park.

After playing his last game at Colchester United in March 1978, he moved to the United States to participate in the growth of the game in that part of the world. He played for Fort Lauderdale in the NASL before later coaching in the States.

PITCH

The Fratton Park pitch measures 114 yards x 72 yards.

PLASTIC

There have been four Football League clubs that have replaced their normal grass playing pitches with artificial surfaces at some stage. Queen's Park Rangers were the first in 1981 but the Loftus Road plastic was discarded in 1988 in favour of a return to turf. Luton Town (1985) Oldham Athletic (1986) and Preston North End (1986) followed.

Portsmouth never played on the Deepdale plastic and though their record on plastic is not a good one, it is probably no worse than that of most clubs. Pompey' first game on plastic was at Boundary Park on 1 November 1986 when they played out a goalless draw with Oldham Athletic.

For their next visit to Oldham in 1988–89, Pompey scored three goals, courtesy of Quinn (two) and Aspinall, but went down 5–3. They scored three goals again the following season with Guy Whittingham hitting a hat-trick in a 3–3 draw. Pompey's last visit to Boundary Park was in the Latic's promotion-winning season of 1990–91 when they were beaten 3–1.

In 1987–88 Pompey played on the Luton Town plastic in the League and League Cup, losing both times 4–1 with Kevin Dillon the scorer on each occasion. Pompey's only game on the Loftus Road plastic was in 1987–88 when they went down 2–1 with Ian Baird the scorer.

PLAY OFFS

In 1992–93 automatic promotion was missed by just one goal in a dramatic final Saturday of the season. Although the club finished level on points with West Ham United, the Hammers secured second spot by courtesy of a single goal.That left Pompey in third position and in the controversial play offs.

After going down 1–0 at Filbert Street in the first leg, Pompey could only draw the home leg 2–2 with McLoughlin and Kristensen the scorers, to go out to a club that finished the season twelve points behind them.

POINTER, RAY

England international centre-forward Ray Pointer made his League debut for Burnley in October 1957, just five days before his twenty-first birthday. During his first full season, he was easily the Claret's top scorer with twenty-seven goals.

In 1959–60 when Burnley won the League Championship, Pointer played in every League and Cup game, scoring twenty-three goals. The goals continued to flow and in 1961 he won the first of three full caps, scoring for England in a 4–1 win over Luxembourg. In April 1963 came the injury that was to signal the beginning of the end of his illustrious Turf Moor career. He chipped a bone in his ankle at Nottingham Forest and two years later after failing to hold down a first team place, he joined Bury.

After scoring seventeen goals in nineteen games for the Gigg Lane club, he was on the move again, this time to Coventry City. With the Sky Blues on their way to promotion for the first time ever, Pointer joined Portsmouth in January 1967.

He was a first team regular at Fratton Park until well into his thirties, by then playing in midfield, when he began combining playing duties with coaching Pompey's youngsters. He played in 165 games for Portsmouth scoring thirty-one goals. He left Fratton Park in the summer of 1973 to team up again with Harry Potts as Blackpool's youth coach, before later returning to Turf Moor as youth team manager.

POINTS

Under the three points for a win system, which was introduced in 1981–82 Portsmouth's best points tally is the ninety-one from forty-six matches in 1982–83 when they won the Third Division championship.

The club's best points tally under the old two points for a win system was sixty-five points from forty-six matches in 1961–62 when Pompey won the Third Division title. This would have netted the club ninety-two points under the present system.

The worst record under either system was the twenty-one points secured in 1958–59 when the club were relegated from the First Division.

POMPEY CHIMES

The unique chant that is delivered to the tune of a chiming clock – 'Play up Pomey, Pompey play up.' The Portsmouth fans repeat the chant over and over again when things are going well for the team.

It has been suggested that Portsmouth's link with chiming clocks may have something to do with the clock in the city's shipyard or else have come about through confusion with the Portsmouth Chines – the town's beaches

POSTPONED

The Second Division match against Clapton Orient at Fratton Park on 13 November 1926 was postponed because the pitch was waterlogged. It was only the fourth time in the club's history that a match had been postponed but the first time a Football League match had suffered that fate.

After drawing 1–1 at home to Scunthorpe United in the third round of the FA Cup on 26 January 1963, Pompey had to endure ten postponements before they could have another go at the Lincolnshire club. Two goals from Ron Saunders in the match played on 7 March took Pompey into the fourth round.

PROMOTION

Portsmouth have been promoted on six occasions. They were first promoted in 1923–24 when they won the Third Divsion (South) championship. Finishing four points ahead of runners-up Plymouth Argyle, Pompey were indebted to Billy Haines who scored twenty-eight goals in thirty games including hat-tricks against Exeter City (Home 4–0), Aberdare Athletic (Home 4–0) and Norwich City (Home 4–0).

Three seasons later, Pompey were promoted to the First Division, finishing as runners-up to Middlesbrough but eight points adrift of the champions. Billy Haines was in even more outstanding form, scoring forty goals in forty-two games. The Warminster-Common born forward scored four goals against Preston North End (Home 5–1) and hat-tricks against Blackpool (Home 5–0) Oldham Athletic (Home 7–2) and Clapton Orient (Away 5–4).

Pompey played First Division football until 1958–59 when they were relegated before dropping into the Third Division two seasons later. Fortunately the club only spent one season in Division Three, winning promotion for the third time as champions in 1961–62. Finishing three points ahead of Grimsby Town, the club's top scorer was Ron Saunders with thirty-two goals, including six doubles.

The club then spent fourteen seasons in the Second Division before dropping into the Third, where two seasons later they finished bottom of the League and so in 1978–79 had to play Fourth Division football for the first time in their history. Two seasons later, the club won promotion for a fourth time, finishing level on points with Bradford City but with a superior goal average.

In 1982–83, Pompey were champions of Division Three, five points ahead of Cardiff City. Alan Biley with twenty-three goals and Billy Rafferty with seventeen, formed a potent strike force. They were last promoted in 1986–87 when they ended the season as runners-up to Derby County, whom they beat 3–1 at Fratton Park courtesy of a Mick Quinn hat-trick.

Q

QUICKEST GOAL

Records do not include precise goal times, so it is an impossible task to state accurately the club's quickest goal scorer. While there have probably been quicker goals, one of the most important early goals was Bill Thompson's twenty second strike in the 5–1 defeat of Aston Villa on 6 May 1950, which resulted in Pompey retaining the League Championship.

QUINN, MICK

An old-fashioned striker, he entered League football with Wigan Athletic, scoring on his debut in a 3–1 win over Halifax Town in April 1980. Although he helped the Latics to promotion to the Third Division, he was released and joined Stockport County. He had scored forty-one goals in seventy League and Cup games for the Edgeley Park side when he was signed by Oldham Athletic.

As with his former clubs, Quinn was the leading goalscorer but in March 1986 the then struggling Lancashire club sold him to Portsmouth for £150,000.

Despite scoring six goals in the last eleven games of the season, Quinn could not help Pompey gain promotion. They made no mistake the following season with Quinn scoring twenty-two goals in the League and six in the Cup competitions, including a hat-trick in a 3–1 win over Derby County. Pompey failed to survive more than one season in the top flight and then fell straight back into the Third Division, but Quinn was top scorer with eighteen League goals.

At the end of his contract, he opted to join Newcastle United, the fee of £680,000 being decided by the Transfer Tribunal. He made a sensational start for the Magpies, scoring four times on his debut against Leeds United and ended the campaign with thirty-two League goals.

In December 1992 after a spell on loan with Coventry City, he joined the Highfield Road club on a permanent basis.

R

RAPID SCORING

In the match against Brighton and Hove Albion at Fratton Park on 31 March 1984, the 12,723 crowd saw Pompey go in at half-time one goal down. In a dramatic second half, the home side scored five goals in a devastating spell to beat the Seagulls 5–1. Portsmouth's scorers were Biley, Dillon, Doyle, Hateley and Webb.

RECEIPTS

The club's record receipts are £214,000 for the Coca Cola Cup fifth round replay against Manchester United on 26 January 1994. A crowd of 24,950 saw Pompey lose 1–0 to a Brian McClair goal.

REID, DUGGIE

Signed from Stockport County in March 1946, Duggie Reid gave great service to the Fratton Park club over the next ten seasons. He scored two goals on his debut in a 3–1 win over Blackburn Rovers on the opening day of the 1946–47 season and went on to end the season as the club's top scorer with twenty-nine goals.

He scored the first of his eight hat-tricks for Pompey in a 3–0 win at Chelsea in May of that season. Despite only playing in thirty-one games in

1947–48, he was again top scorer with fourteen goals, netting three of them in the 6–0 home win over Grimsby Town.

In 1948–49, the club's first Championship-winning season, Reid again missed a number of matches through injury but was still joint top scorer with Peter Harris with seventeen goals, including another hat-trick against Charlton Athletic. He was only able to turn out in twenty-seven League games in the following season when Pompey retained the title, but he scored sixteen goals, including hat-tricks in the defeat of Everton (Home 7–0) Chelsea (Home 4–0) and Aston Villa (Home 5–1). In 1950–51 he top scored again with twenty-one goals in the League.

Reid scored Pompey's only goals in the first three fixtures of the season which all ended in 1–1 draws and a hat-trick in a 4–1 win at Chelsea. His prolific goalscoring continued in 1951–52 when he top scored with sixteen goals from just thirty matches. A great team man, he deputised for Froggatt in the heart of defence and on one occasion went in goal when Platt was injured.

He played the last of his 327 first team games, in which he had scored 135 goals, on 28 April 1956 before joining Tonbridge. He later returned to Fratton Park to become groundsman at the club's new Tamworth Road training ground.

REILLY, MATT

Although he had played Gaelic football back home in Ireland, it was when playing in Army football that the goalkeeper first came to prominence. He spent four years with the Royal Artillery in the Southern League and also made two appearances in that competition for Southampton in 1895–96 as a 'guest' player. With the demise of the Royal Artillery at the end of the 1897–98 season, Portsmouth were founded and Reilly became the club's first goalkeeper.

A regular for the next six seasons, he helped Pompey win the Southern League title in 1901–02 and played for Ireland against England in March 1900 and again in March 1902. In January 1904, the match against Swindon which Portsmouth won 1–0 was interrupted by crowd trouble and the hot-headed Irishman, angry at being bombarded by clinker, hit one of the culprits and was suspended for two weeks.

In the summer of 1904, he moved to Dundee but after just one season, joined Notts County. At the end of the 1905–06 season, he was released and joined Spurs.

He later returned to Ireland to play for Shelbourne. In later life he became a publican at Southsea and he died at his home in Donnybrook, Dublin, in December 1954, aged eighty.

RELEGATION

Portsmouth have been relegated on five occasions. Their first taste came in 1958–59 when they finished bottom of the First Division after twenty-five years in the top flight. It was a season in which the club conceded 112 goals and suffered some heavy defeats – Wolverhampton Wanderers (Away 0–7), West Ham United (Away 0–6), Manchester United (Away 1–6) and West Bromwich Albion (Home 2–6).

Two seasons later, Pompey were relegated from the Second to the Third Division and though they bounced straight back as champions, they were relegated for a third time in 1975–76 after fourteen seasons of Second Division football.

Relegation to the Fourth Division for the first time in the club's history came at the end of the 1977–78 season when Pompey finished bottom of Division Three. Over the next eight seasons Pompey won promotion three times and in 1987–88 played First Division football.

The club's last experience of relegation came one season later when after finishing third from bottom in the top flight they returned to the Second Division.

ROYAL ARTILLERY

Formed in 1894 out of an amalgamation between 15th Company RA (Fareham) and Depot RA (Portsmouth) their existence was brief. Being a military side, they were led by Sergeant Major Windrum and Sergeant Richard Bonney, who was later connected with Portsmouth, a club formed after the demise of the Royal Artillery.

After winning the Army Cup in 1895 and 1897 and the Hampshire Cup in 1896, when they also reached the final of the English Amateur Cup, where they lost to Bishop Auckland, they decided to apply for election to the Second Division of the Southern League. They won the title at their first attempt with an impressive nineteen victories in twenty-two matches and, after a series of Test Matches, won promotion. They struggled in the First Division of the Southern League, winning only four of their twenty-four matches, yet had a fine run in the FA Amateur Cup.

Disaster struck after a tie against Harwich and Parkeston. The team spent the preceding week training at Alderbury on the east coast. The Cup committee later felt that billiards, cigars and wine, paid for by the club, were a little beyond their ideas of amateurism. They ejected the Royal Artillery and suspended the players for professionalism. The club never recovered and their place was taken by newly formed Portsmouth FC the following season.

RUGBY UNION

Following their promotion from the Third Division (South), Portsmouth decided to stage Rugby Union games at Fratton Park during the 1924–25 Second Division season. One such game saw Hampshire play hosts to the All Blacks touring team. In a fairly one-sided game, the New Zealanders won 22–0.

S

SAUNDERS, RON

Ron Saunders played for Birkenhead and Liverpool Schools before signing for Everton in 1951. Much was expected of him when he gained Youth International honours but he never established himself at the top level. After making just three appearances for the Goodison Park club he moved to non-League Tonbridge. His League career was rescued by Gillingham who signed him in May 1957.

After twenty goals in forty-nine League appearances for the Gills, Portsmouth saw his potential and signed him for £8,000 in September 1958. He ended that season as the club's top scorer with twenty-one goals in thirty-six appearances including a hat-trick in a 4–4 draw at Tottenham Hotspur. He was the club's leading scorer in each of his six seasons at

Fratton Park and in 1961–62 when Pompey won the Third Division championship, he scored thirty-two goals. However, his best season in terms of goals scored was 1963–64 when he netted thirty-three goals, including hat-tricks in successive matches – Newcastle United (Home 5–2) and Leyton Orient (Away 6–3). He also scored a hat-trick in the home match against Leyton Orient as Pompey won 4–3.

Saunders scored 162 League and Cup goals for Portsmouth in 261 games before moving to Watford in September 1964 for £15,000. He was later transferred to Charlton Athletic.

He started on the road to management with non-League Yeovil Town before taking charge at Oxford United and later Norwich City. At Carrow Road, he led the club to the Second Division championship and to the League Cup Final. After a bitter row in the boardroom he left Norwich for Manchester City but lasted just five months at Maine Road before taking control at Aston Villa.

He transformed a disappointing Villa side into League Cup winners and runners-up in the Second Division in his first season in charge. In 1980–81 he led the club to the League Championship and this qualified Villa for the following season's European Cup. They had reached the quarter-finals before Saunders surprisingly resigned. He later managed Birmingham City and West Bromwich Albion before leaving the game.

SCORES: HIGHEST

Portsmouth's highest score in any first team match was their 16–1 win at home to Clapton Orient on 28 February 1942 in a London War League game. Andy Black of Hearts was 'guesting' for Pompey in this match and scored eight goals.

Cowes were beaten 12–0 on 6 April 1918 in a South Hants War League game and the following season, Pompey beat the Royal Engineers 11–0 in the same competition.

The club's best victory in the FA Cup came against Ryde on 30 September 1899, when the Isle of Wight side were beaten 10–0 with Sandy Brown and William Smith both netting hat-tricks.

In the Football League, Notts County were beaten 9–1 in a Second Division match in 1926–27.

SCOULAR, JIMMY

Born in Livingston, near Edinburgh, the son of a miner, Jimmy Scoular became a steel-foundry worker on leaving school and always had a keen interest in football. His father had played in the Scottish League for a number of clubs and at fourteen Jimmy was following in his footsteps being capped by his county and reaching Scottish Schoolboy international trials.

He won junior caps before joining the Royal Navy in 1943 when he was posted 500 miles away from home – to HMS *Dolphin* near Portsmouth. He played for Gosport Borough and for the Navy team.

Both Southampton and Portsmouth showed an interest in the seventeen year old Scot but it was Pompey who secured his signature. In December 1945, he signed professional forms for the Fratton Park club but could not devote his attentions to full-time football until his demobilisation a year later. For almost seven seasons he was part of a great half-back line of Scoular/Flewin/Dickinson, the backbone of Portsmouth's League Championship victories of 1948–49 and 1949–50.

Nicknamed 'Ironman' by the press, Scoular had an unshakable will to win. He was always in the thick of the action and was sent off a few times, including the first match of the club's South American tour of 1951.

He won nine Scotland caps while at Fratton Park, the first in a 3–1 win over Denmark in 1951. After appearing in 264 League and Cup games for Pompey, he moved to Newcastle United for £22,250.

Appointed captain, he skippered the Magpies to Wembley in 1955 and helped bring the FA Cup to Tyneside for the third time in five seasons. He had played in 271 League and Cup games for Newcastle when he accepted the player-manager's job at Bradford Park Avenue. He took them to Division Three and then saw the club relegated two years later.

Scoular finally hung up his boots in March 1964 and later that year became manager of Cardiff City, a position he filled for nine years. A brief stay with Newport County followed until he left the manager's merry-go-round in January 1978.

SECOND DIVISION

Portsmouth have had five spells in the Second Division. Their first season in the Second Division was 1924–25 following their promotion as champions of the Third Division (South) the previous season. They won their first ever match in this division 2–0 at South Shields and ended that first campaign in fourth position. After finishing mid-table in 1925–26, Pompey were promoted to Division One the following season, finishing as runners-up to Middlesbrough. It was during this season that the club produced their best League victory, beating Notts County 9–1.

The club's second spell in the Second Division lasted just two seasons, 1959–60 and 1960–61. After they had spent twenty-five seasons in Division One. The Fratton Park club only just avoided immediate relegation to the Third Division in that season of 1959–60 but the following season not even a win in the last game against Derby County could prevent them dropping into Division Three.

However, Pompey bounced back immediately as champions of the Third Division and then spent their longest spell in the Second Division of fourteen seasons. Their best position during this third spell in Division Two was fifth in 1967–68.

Relegated in 1975–76, the club went down to the Fourth Division for the first time in their history two seasons later and spent two seasons in the basement before returning to the Third Division. After winning the Third Division championship in 1982–83, Pompey embarked on their fourth spell in the Second Division and after finishing fourth in seasons 1984–85 and 1985–86, were promoted to the First Division in 1986–87 where they finished second to Derby County, their success based on a sound defence in which goalkeeper Alan Knight kept twenty clean sheets.

Unfortunately, Pompey were relegated after just one season in the top flight and at the time of writing are still playing 'Second' Division football although following reorganisation in 1992–93, it is now known as the First Division. The club's best position in this last spell in this divsion is third in 1992–93 when Guy Whittingham scored forty-two goals.

SIMOD CUP

The Simod Cup replaced the Full Members' Cup for the 1987–88 season. Portsmouth's first match in the competition saw them go down 3–0 at home to Second Division Stoke City in front of a 3,226 crowd, with Bill Gilbert putting through his own goal.

In 1988–89 Portsmouth beat Hull City 2–1 with Quinn and Hardyman the scorers, before losing by the same scoreline at Middlesbrough

SMALLEST PLAYER

Although such statistics are always unreliable for those playing before the turn of the century, the distinction of being Pompey's smallest player goes to outside-right Ray Wilde. One of the smallest players of all time, he stood just 5ft 2 ins.

SMITH, GEORGE

Centre-half George Smith played for Charlton Athletic during the war years and appeared in an FA Cup Final against Chelsea at Wembley in 1944, which Athletic won 3–1. In May 1945, he gained a wartime cap for England against Wales. After the hostilities, he joined Queen's Park Rangers and won a Third Division (South) championship medal with the Loftus Road club in 1947–48.

After a good number of years managing non-League clubs, he took charge at Crystal Palace, saying that he would resign after two years if he did not get them promoted. When he failed to do so, he kept his promise and spent twelve months as Sheffield United's coach before taking over the reins at Fratton Park. He took Portsmouth to the Third Division championship in 1961–62 at the end of his first season in charge.

In the summer of 1965, he made a number of radical changes, including scrapping the reserve side and only having sixteen professionals in an attempt to save money. In April 1970 he became the club's general manager, but three years later he lost his job when Pompey's new chairman, John Deacon, reconstructed the club's management.

SMITH, JACK

Having made his mark with North Shields Athletic during the First World War, he joined South Shields for just £5 in 1919. He played in more than 150 games for the club before moving to Portsmouth in 1928.

Jack Smith made his debut for Pompey on 21 January 1928, scoring both goals in a 2–1 win over West Ham United. Three games later he scored a hat-trick but was on the losing side as Pompey went down 5–3 at home to Sunderland. He ended that season with eleven goals in eighteen League games. The following season, the club reached its first FA Cup Final at Wembley, with Smith scoring the only goal of the semi-final against Aston Villa.

Regarded by many as Portsmouth's leading tactician, he won his first international cap against Ireland in 1931 at the age of thirty-three. He scored one of England's goals in a 6–2 Belfast win. His two other international caps came later that same year against Wales at Liverpool, when he scored once in a 3–1 win and against Spain at Highbury when he scored twice in a famous 7–1 England victory.

It was said that Jack Smith wore very large shin pads, but they certainly did not inhibit the passing skills of an inside-right who scored sixty-nine League and Cup goals in 289 games. At the end of the 1934–35 season, he left Fratton Park to play for Bournemouth.

SMITH, JIM

Known as the 'Bald Eagle', Jim Smith played all his football in the Fourth Division for Aldershot, Halifax and Lincoln. In 1969 he became player-manager of non-League Boston United, where he gained a reputation as a shrewd manager. Attracted by his work at Boston, Colchester United appointed him their manager. He took the Layer Road club to third in the Fourth Division and promotion, as well as reaching the quarter-finals of the League Cup.

In the summer of 1975, Blackburn Rovers came in with a lucrative offer for Smith and though his sides played exciting, attacking football, they never challenged for promotion to the First Division. He then took charge at Birmingham City but at the end of his first full season the St Andrews club were relegated to the Second Division. In 1979–80 they finished third in Division Two and so bounced straight back to the top flight, but after two mediocre seasons, he was sacked.

He was not out of work for long, being appointed manager of Oxford United. The Manor Ground club came close to promotion twice before winning the Third Division championship in 1984. Smith then took United to the Second Division championship the following season but amazed everybody by moving to Queen's Park Rangers. He led the Loftus Road club to the League Cup Final, where they lost 3–0 to Oxford United.

In December 1988 he joined Newcastle United but after becoming tired of the minefield of politics, resigned to take up a coaching post at Middlesbrough.

In the summer of 1991 he took over at Fratton Park. He had an excellent first season, taking the club to the semi-finals of the FA Cup, where they lost to Liverpool in a penalty shoot-out after two drawn games. In 1992–93 the club were unlucky to miss automatic promotion but then lost to Leicester City in the play-offs.

In February 1995, Smith was sacked and after a spell as chief executive of the League Managers' Association, he took charge at Derby County, guiding them into the Premiership at the end of the 1995–96 season.

SMITH, STEVE

England international Steve Smith began his career with Aston Villa, where he won five League Championship medals and two FA Cup winners' medals. His one and only international appearance was against Scotland at Goodison Park in 1895 when he scored one of the goals in a 3–0 win. After scoring forty-two goals in 191 games, he left Villa for Portsmouth.

In his first season at Fratton Park, he helped

the club win the Southern League title, scoring six goals in twenty-one appearances. The brother of Billy Smith, who had been one of Frank Brettell's first signings, he went on to appear in 230 games for Pompey, scoring twenty-two goals before later becoming player-manager of New Brompton (Gillingham).

SMITH, WILLIAM

Left-back William Smith followed his brother, Jack, to Fratton Park from South Shields in 1928 and made his debut in a goal-less draw against Manchester United at Old Trafford in the final game of the 1928–29 season.

By 1930, he had made the Number 3 shirt his own and over the next seven seasons, missed just five games, being an ever-present in seasons 1930–31 and 1933–34.

He appeared in 335 League and Cup games for Pompey, scoring just two goals. They came in the 2–2 draw at Sheffield Wednesday in April 1931 and in a 2–1 reversal at Leicester City in February 1932. He played the last game of his nine year Pompey career at Leeds United on the final day of the 1936–37 season, later ending his career with Stockport County.

SOUTHAMPTON

Portsmouth's arch rivals are Southampton, who are commonly labelled 'Scrummers' by the Pompey faithful.

The two clubs first met on 5 September 1899 at Fratton Park when goals from Danny Cunliffe and Harold 'Nobby' Clarke gave Portsmouth a 2–0 win. They met many times in a variety of competitions before they both entered the Third Division of the Football League.

In 1915–16, Pompey won 7–0 with Frank Stringfellow netting a hat-trick. In the South Hants War League of 1918–19 the clubs met three times, Pompey winning two of the meetings 5–3 and 6–3 but losing the third 9–1.

Their first meeting in the Football League was on 11 September 1920 when Southampton won 2–0 at The Dell. The Saints completed the double a week later, winning 1–0 at Fratton Park.

The first time Pompey completed the double over their rivals was 1926–27 when they won promotion to the First Division. They won the opening game of the season 3–1 with goals from Haines, Goodwin and McKenzie and the return at The Dell 2–0 with two goals from Billy Haines.

The two clubs did not meet again for thirty-four years and when they did, Southampton won their home match 5–1.

In 1963–64, Pompey did the double a second time, winning 2–0 at Fratton Park and 3–2 at The Dell.

Their last meeting was in the 1987–88 season – the only time they have met in the top flight. They shared the points in a 2–2 draw at Fratton Park and then goals from Barry Horne and Terry Connor gave Pompey a 2–0 victory away from home.

SOUTHERN ALLIANCE

Pompey played in the Southern Alliance in the seasons of 1912–13 and 1913–14. During their first season in the competition they won seven and drew two of their sixteen fixtures. J Love Jones, who later died while on Pompey's books, scored a hat-trick in the 3–0 win over Luton. The following season Pompey won six and lost the other ten of the sixteen matches, conceding four goals on three occasions.

SOUTHERN DISTRICT COMBINATION

Portsmouth competed in the Southern District Combination for one season only, that of 1899–1900. After losing their first match at Tottenham 2–0, they won their first game at Fratton Park, beating Chatham 4–1. Winning eight and drawing two of their sixteen matches, they ended the season in third place.

SOUTHERN LEAGUE

Portsmouth's first Southern League fixture was at Chatham on 2 September 1899. Harold 'Nobby' Clarke, the twenty-four year old winger, scored Pompey's historic first goal in a 1–0 victory. The club went on to win twenty of their twenty-eight League games and ended the season three points behind champions, Tottenham Hotspur.

Portsmouth then lost some of their star players in the close season, due to the high price of their new Fratton Park ground. It cost £6,538 to buy, with stands, dressing rooms, committee rooms and turnstiles costing a further £9,372.

Frank Bedlingfield was bought from Queen's Park Rangers to replace the departing Sandy Brown to Spurs. He scored thirty goals in all matches for Portsmouth that season.

The 1901–02 season saw Portsmouth's first Southern League championship. The club dropped only thirteen points out of a possible sixty, winning twenty games in their march to the title. They were five points clear of their nearest rivals, Spurs and Southampton. One of the 'crunch' games was the club's 1–0 victory at Fratton Park against Tottenham on 31 March 1902 when a Billy Smith penalty separated the teams in front of 13,408 – the biggest crowd of the season.

Bob Blyth, later to become the club chairman, took over as manager in place of Frank Brettell. He signed internationals Steve Smith from Aston Villa and Arthur Chadwick from Southampton. The leading goal scorer was Danny Cunliffe with eighteen goals, yet Frank Bedlingfield had scored twenty-five goals by February before collapsing in the dressing room after the FA Cup game against Reading with consumption. His replacement was Alex McDonald and he hit four goals in Pompey's biggest win of the season, 7–1 against Brentford in April.

On 18 October 1902, Northampton became the first side to visit Fratton Park and win. Though they failed to defend their championship, the club had a powerful squad with nine internationals on the staff.

After finishing third in 1905–06, Pompey signed Southampton star Jack Warner, Scottish international full-back Jimmy Thomson and Irish international Harry Buckle from Sunderland. They ended the season as runners-up to Fulham and when the two clubs met on 15 February 1907, a massive crowd of more than 30,000 saw Fulham win 2–0 at Craven Cottage.

There followed a few seasons of comparative mediocrity before the club finished runners-up in 1911–12. Despite the outbreak of the First World War in August 1914 there was a full Southern League programme with Pompey finishing in seventh place.

The club's last season in the Southern League was 1919–20 when they won their second championship. Though they made most of the running they only took the title on goal average. Pompey only needed to beat lowly Newport County in their last match but were beaten 1–0, leaving Watford who beat Southampton 3–0 to also finish with fifty-eight points. The championship trophy came to Fratton Park on the strength of the club's superior goal average.

SOUTH HANTS WAR LEAGUE

Pompey spent the 1917–18 and 1918–19 seasons playing in this competition following the decision of the London clubs not to travel to Portsmouth or Southampton.

In 1917–18, the club won 12 of its 13 matches, losing only one 2–0 to Wooston. The victories included Cowes 12–0 and the School of Flying 9–0. The following season saw Pompey win ten and draw three of their seventeen matches, gaining revenge over Th'crofts Woolston by winning 10–2 with Joseph Turner scoring five of the goals.

SPONSORS

Pompey's official club sponsor is K J C Mobile Phones.

ST JOHN, IAN

Ian St John began his playing career with Motherwell and once scored a hat-trick for the Fir Park club inside two and a half minutes. In May 1961 he joined Liverpool for £37,500 and scored a superb headed goal when the Anfield side beat Leeds United in the FA Cup Final of 1965.

He made 424 appearances for Liverpool, scoring 118 goals before leaving to join Coventry City. He later had a short spell with Tranmere Rovers before entering management with Motherwell. After just one season in charge, in which Motherwell finished seventh in Division One, he moved south to manage Portsmouth.

The club had huge debts of around £300,000 and so St John had very little money to spend. Things became so desperate at one stage that he had to blood youth team players like Steve Foster and Chris Kamara straight into the first team.

The entire Portsmouth board resigned and St John was sacked with the club perilously close to relegation to the Fourth Division. He later worked as a television presenter, appearing on the *Saint and Greavsie Show*.

STRINGFELLOW, FRANK

Born in Sutton-in-Ashfield, inside-right Frank Stringfellow joined Portsmouth from Sheffield Wednesday in the summer of 1911. He was brought to Fratton Park along with Michael Dowling by Bob Brown.

Standing just 5ft 5ins, Stringfellow was one of the smallest players ever to be a regular in the Pompey side. He made his debut in the 11–0 win over Chesham in the Southern League Second Division on the opening day of the 1911–12 season.

A fairly consistent goal scorer, he notched his first hat-trick for the club in the 1915–16 season when Pompey beat Southampton 7–0 in a friendly. He followed this with a second hat-trick in the London Combination match against Queen's Park Rangers in December 1916, which Pompey won 7–1.

In 1919–20, Stringfellow was an ever-present as the club won the Southern League championship, top-scoring with twenty goals. The following season, the club's first in the Football League, he ended the campaign as Pompey's leading scorer with thirteen League goals. Although he only played in twenty-three matches in 1921–22, he again scored thirteen goals, including seven in his last six games for the club.

He left Fratton Park to join Hearts but two years later moved to new Southern League club Weymouth, for £1,000.

SUBSTITUTES

The first playing Portsmouth substitute was Tony Barton who came on for Vince Radcliffe against Southampton at The Dell on 28 August 1965 in a 2–2 draw. The club had to wait until 2 December 1967 for their first goalscoring substitute – Micky Travers, who scored in the 3–1 home win over Blackpool.

The greatest number of substitutes used in a single season by Portsmouth under the single substitute rule was 33 in 1978–79 but since 1986–87, two substitutes have been allowed and in 1991–92, 83 were used.

From 1995–96 three substitute's were allowed and in 1996–97 ninety-seven were used.

The greatest number of substitute appearances for Portsmouth has been made by Paul Wood who came on during twenty-nine League games with five more in cup ties. It was in 1995–96 that Sammy Igoe rewrote the Pompey records on the matter of substitutes with an extraordinary eighteen League appearances in the substitute's shirt, a total both he and John Durnin equalled in 1996–97.

SUNDAY FOOTBALL

The first Sunday matches in the Football League took place on 20 January 1974 as a result of the three day week imposed by the government during its trial of strength with the coalminers. On Sunday 27 January, a crowd of 32,838 turned up at Fratton Park to see Pompey play out a goal-less draw with Leyton Orient in the fourth round of the FA Cup.

A week later, Portsmouth played their first League match on a Sunday when they entertained West Bromwich Albion. A goal by Norman Piper gave Pompey a 1–1 draw. After beating Leyton Orient 2–0 in the replay, Pompey travelled to Nottingham Forest for the fifth round tie on Sunday 17 February, only to lose 1–0 to a Duncan McKenzie penalty.

During the 1980–81 season, the club decided to test public reaction to League football on a Sunday and moved their match against Oxford United back twenty-four hours. The gate of 12,243 was no more than average and so the club decided against a break from tradition.

SUPERSTITIONS

Portsmouth manager Jack Tinn wore a pair of lucky white spats throughout his team's 1939 FA Cup run. It certainly worked because Pompey surprisingly beat Wolverhampton Wanderers 4–1 in the final. Fred Worrall, the Pompey winger had to fasten them on match days throughout the club's success that year. He became tired of the ritual but Tinn always insisted.

Yet Worralll had his own superstitions. He always played with a sixpence (2 p) in his boot and a miniature horseshoe in his pocket. Down each stocking he pushed a sprig of white heather and he tied a small white elephant to one of his garters.

SUPPORTERS CLUB

Portsmouth Supporters Club was formed in October 1929 by Percy Mabb and Colour Sergeant F.Brimer. But after seven years in which the membership had dropped from around 1,700 to 143, the club disbanded. Happily, only a month elapsed before they re-formed. The Supporters Club continued to go from strength to strength, yet it was only during the 1958–59 season that Pompey officials recognised it.

SUSPENSIONS

In May 1950, the club's chairman, Vernon Stokes, and director, Harry Wain, were suspended *sine die* for irregularities over the return of Irish international Jimmy McAlinden from Ireland. There was also an alleged payment of £750 to McAlinden, who was suspended from playing until 1 October, while Pompey manager Jack Tinn was censured and the Fratton Park club fined £750.

In February of the following year, after receiving a 25,000 signature petition from Pompey's Supporters Club and having re-considered the evidence, the FA lifted the ban on Vernon Stokes and Harry Wain and they were reinstated.

SUSTAINED SCORING

During the 1926–27 season, when Pompey won promotion to the First Division, Billy Haines scored forty goals in forty-two League appearances, including four in the final game of the season in a 5–1 home win over Preston North End and hat-tricks against Blackpool (Home 5–0) Oldham Athletic (Home 7–2) and Clapton Orient (Away 5–4).

In 1992–93, when the club finished third in the newly formed First Division, Guy Whittingham scored forty-two goals in forty-six League games, including all four goals in the 4–1 Boxing Day win over Bristol Rovers at Fratton Park and hat-tricks against Bristol City (Away 3-3) on the opening day of the season, Luton Town (Away 4–1) and Peterborough United (Home 4–0).

SWAIN, KENNY

The Birkenhead-born player started his League career with Chelsea, scoring nineteen goals in 126 outings for the Stamford Bridge club before moving to Aston Villa in December 1978. At Villa Park, he was converted into a right-back and won medals for League Championship, European Cup and European Cup successes in seasons 1980–81 and 1981–82. He had played 178 first team games for Villa before joining Nottingham Forest in 1983.

He signed for Portsmouth in the summer of 1985 and made his debut in a 2–2 draw at Hull City on the opening day of the 1985–86 season. After playing in thirty-nine games that season, he was an ever-present in 1986–87 helping Pompey win promotion to the First Division. He had a spell on loan at West Bromwich Albion but after playing in 134 games for the Fratton Park club, he joined Crewe Alexandra as player-coach.

He appeared in 625 League games for his six clubs before being appointed manager of Wigan Athletic in 1993.

SYMONS, KIT

A highly rated central defender, he joined Portsmouth straight from school as a trainee and quickly became captain of the Youth side before being given his League debut by Alan Ball in a 2–1 defeat at Leicester City in January 1989.

However, up until the start of the 1991–92 season, he had only played in four League games for the Fratton Park club. That season, he was an ever-present, scored his first goal for the club in a 2–0 win over Barnsley on the final day of the season and was voted Pompey's Player of the Year.

A seasoned Welsh international with twenty-two caps to his name, he had played in 190 League and Cup games for Pompey when former boss Alan Ball, then in charge at Manchester City, took him to Maine Road at the beginning of the 1995–96 season.

T

TAIT, MICK

Born in Wallsend, Mick Tait was signed by Oxford United after playing for Wallsend Boys Club against Oxford Boys and made his League debut for the Manor Ground club in February 1975. He went on to appear in sixty-nine League and Cup games before financial difficulties and dwindling attendances forced United to sell him to Carlisle United for their record fee of £65,000. He later joined Hull City for another club record fee of £150,000.

Only nine months later, the combative Tait, who liked to play as a deep lying forward, making runs from the halfway line and finishing them off with a powerful shot, joined Pompey for £100,000. He spent seven seasons at Fratton Park, scoring thirty-one goals in 278 League and Cup appearances and featuring in the club's Third Division championship and Second Division promotion sides.

The strong-tackling midfield man later signed for Reading and was a member of their 1987–88 Simod Cup winning side.

TALLEST PLAYER

It is impossible to say for sure who has been the tallest player on Portsmouth's books as such records are notoriously unreliable. But almost certain to lay claim to the distinction is 6ft 4 ins goalkeeper Andy Gosney, who between 1981 and 1991 made forty-eight League appearances for Pompey.

TELEVISION

Portsmouth have appeared on BBC's *Match of the Day* on a good number of occasions, the first being on 25 February 1967 when, despite two goals from Cliff Portwood, they went down 3–2 to Wolverhampton Wanderers in front of a Fratton Park crowd of 23,144, the biggest of the season.

THACKERAY, DAVID

Born at Hamilton, David Thackeray played for Alloa and Motherwell before entering English football with Portsmouth in 1928. The burly left-half made his debut for the Fratton Park club in a 1–0 win over Huddersfield Town in the opening game of the 1928–29 season. At the end of that campaign, he had missed just two matches and played in the FA Cup Final against Bolton Wanderers.

Thackeray brought all the art and craft of Scottish football to his game and was a big factor in building Pompey's fortunes. He secured a second FA Cup losers' medal when he was in the side that lost to Manchester City in 1934. Although he was often in the running for a Scottish cap, he was unfortunate in not being picked for an international match.

He played the last of his 308 games for Portsmouth in a 3–2 win over Sheffield Wednesday in September 1935 before retiring from the game.

THIRD DIVISION

Portsmouth have had four spells in the Third Division. Their first season in League football in 1920–21 saw them finish twelfth in the Third Division with thirty-nine points as the title went to Crystal Palace. The following season, there was a marked improvement and Pompey ended the season in third place behind champions Southampton and runners-up Plymouth Argyle. The club finished seventh in 1922–23 but in their fourth season, they won the Third Division championship with fifty-nine points, four more than runners-up Plymouth Argyle.

Pompey's second spell in the Third Division lasted just one season. Relegated at the end of the 1960–61 season, they bounced back straightaway as champions with sixty-five points. They made a good start, winning eight and drawing six of their first fourteen fixtures and were beaten for the first time on 7 October by Notts County at Meadow Lane, 2–1. Despite only picking up one point in a five match spell towards the end of the season, Portsmouth won the title when they beat Watford 2–1 at Fratton Park with still two games to play.

The club's third spell in the Third Division lasted two seasons. Following relegation in 1975–76, Pompey looked to be heading to the Fourth

Division before rallying to finish twentieth. However, in 1977–78, they finished bottom of the Third Division with thirty-one points and were relegated to the League's basement for the first time in their history.

Pompey's fourth and final spell in the Third Division lasted three seasons. After winning promotion in 1979–80, the club finished sixth and thirteenth in the two seasons before winning the Third Division championship in 1982–83 with ninety-one points, five points ahead of runners-up, Cardiff City.

TINDALL, RON

A tall and speedy centre-forward, Ron Tindall began his League career with Chelsea and scored seventy goals in 172 games before moving to Upton Park. Unable to win a regular first team place with West Ham, he joined Reading before later signing for Portsmouth.

He made his debut for Pompey in a 1–0 defeat at Rotherham United in September 1964. He went on to appear in 180 League and Cup games for the club, showing his versatility by wearing nine different numbered shirts, though most of his appearances were at full-back.

Tindall was also an excellent cricketer. An all-rounder, he appeared in 172 games for Surrey between 1956 and 1966. When he took over as Portsmouth manager, following George Smith's move to general manager, he soon enetered the transfer market, splashing out £40,000 on Plymouth Argyle's Norman Piper and at the end of the season, signing goalkeeper Jim Standen from West Ham United.

At this time, Portsmouth did not have a reserve side and so Tindall adopted Southern League outfit, Waterlooville, as a nursery side. Unfortunately, during his term of management, Pompey incurred large debts and he was allowed to spend more than was wise on new players.

In 1973, he became general manager, allowing John Mortimore to take charge of team affairs, but a year later he was suspended and Tindall was appointed on a caretaker basis until the arrival of Ian St John.

TINN, JACK

Little is known about Jack Tinn's early life. He did not play professional football and was forty-two years of age when he became involved in top class soccer as manager of his home town club, South Shields. He was forced to sell his better players so that the club could survive and when he left the north-east to manage Portsmouth in July 1927, the club went into decline.

The Fratton Park club had just been promoted to the First Division when Tinn took control. They just avoided relegation in his first two seasons in charge but in 1929, Tinn took them to Wembley. Here, Pompey lost 2–0 to favourites Bolton Wanderers after holding out for seventy-eight minutes. In 1930–31 he introduced some better players and the club finished fourth in the First Division.

They were back at Wembley again in 1934 but lost 2–1 to Manchester City after Rutherford had given them the lead. Tinn finally took Pompey to a winning Cup Final in 1939 as Wolverhampton Wanderers were beaten 4–1.

Tinn was also famous for wearing his lucky spats, which were religiously put on by the same player before every match.

Although he managed to keep Pompey in the First Division, they usually struggled near the foot of the table. It was around this time that Tinn came in for some heavy criticism but this was a little unfair as he had brought much success to Fratton Park, especially in the FA Cup. He resigned in May 1947.

TOURS

Portsmouth have undertaken a number of overseas tours. Their first was to Germany and Austria in 1907 and in the match against Leipzig, Bill 'Sunny Jim' Kirby scored four goals in Pompey's 6–1 win and against Dresden, new signing Randall hit a hat-trick.

The club's biggest overseas tour was a three week trip to South America at the end of the 1950–51 season. In the opening match Jimmy Scoular was sent off in a 2–1 defeat by Fluminese in front of a 200,000 crowd. Pompey then lost 3–2 to Brazil's leading side America and 4–0 to Santos but drew 1–1 with Sao Paolo and 0–0 with Palmeiras, who went on to become champions of Brazil.

TRANSFERS

The club's record transfer fee received is £1.7 million from Tottenham Hotspur for Darren Anderton. The club's only other incoming fee for £1 million was for Mark Hately from Inter Milan in the summer of 1984. The club's record transfer fee paid is £500,000 to Celtic for Gerry Creaney in January 1994.

TREBILCOCK, MIKE

Less than four months after joining Everton from Plymouth Argyle for 20,000, the little Cornishman was drafted into the FA Cup semi-final against Manchester United, replacing Fred Pickering. Rather surprisingly, he kept his place for the final against Sheffield Wednesday. Everton were 2–0 down when in the space of six minutes, Trebilcock scored twice with stunning shots, leaving Derek Temple to complete one of the FA Cup Final's greatest fightbacks. It proved to be his last game for Everton for after two years on Merseyside and only eleven League games, he joined Portsmouth.

   He scored against Derby County in a 3–2 win on his home debut and the only goal of the game in a 1–0 FA Cup fourth round replay win over Fulham. Manager George Smith saw Trebilcock as the striker who would add goals to the club's promotion push but they did not come as often as the fans would have liked.

In fact, during his 122 games games for Pompey, there was only one occasion when Trebilcock looked like living up to his scoring reputation. In October 1970, he hit hat-tricks in a 5–0 win over Watford and a 4–1 defeat of Blackburn Rovers.

A figure of controversy during his time at Fratton Park, he joined Torquay United in the summer of 1972 before later emigrating to Australia.

UNDEFEATED

Portsmouth have remained undefeated at home throughout just one League season. In 1948–49 they won eighteen and drew three of their home matches in winning the First Division title.

The club's best and longest undefeated home sequence in the Football League is of thirty-two matches between 3 January 1948 and 27 August 1949. Portsmouth's longest run of undefeated Football League matches home and away is fifteen between 18 April 1924 and 18 October 1924.

UNUSUAL GOALS

One of the most unusual goals seen at Fratton Park occurred on 13 September 1941 when Pompey entertained Aldershot in the London War League.

The visitors side, which included the entire England half-back line of Britton, Cullis and Mercer, were 2–1 ahead with ten minutes remaining. Cliff Parker collected the ball on the halfway line and made his way down the left hand touchline. As he cut in, Andy Black, the Scottish international who was 'guesting' for Pompey, made his way into the penalty area.

Parker was about thirty yards from goal when he flighted the ball towards the top corner of the net. It appeared as if Andy Black would make contact with the ball, but it dipped viciously under the bar. Black was unable to stop himself and as the ball entered the net, he headed the crossbar before ending up in the back of the net. The post snapped at the base and because the groundsman was unable to repair it, the game was abandoned with the score of 2–2 being allowed to stand.

UPRICHARD, NORMAN

Signed from Swindon Town in November 1952, the Irish goalkeeper marked his debut with an own goal against Spurs but had the last laugh as Pompey won 2–1.

His second game for the club against Sheffield Wednesday at Hillsborough was also dramatic in that with Portsmouth leading 4–3, Uprichard suffered smashed knuckles in a last minute unsighted clash with Derek Dooley. Happily he recovered and returned to the Pompey side by Christmas, wearing a special padded glove.

Although he was only a small 'keeper, the Irishman soon won over the Portsmouth crowd. Renowned for his bravery, he became famous for his one on one saves and also for punching the ball out among a crowd of players. Known as 'Black Jake' his popularity was such that he needed his goalkeeper's cap to collect all the sweets thrown to him during warm ups before games.

A Northern Ireland international, he won eighteen full caps for his country and appeared in the 1958 World Cup Finals in Sweden. It was against Czechoslovakia in this competition, that he played for seventy minutes with a broken hand, but still helped the Irish win 2–1.

Despite suffering from a catalogue of injuries during his seven year stay with Portsmouth, he appeared in 191 League and Cup games for the club. Once, when he was not fit to keep goal, he played on the wing for the Reserves and scored two goals.

He left Fratton Park for Southend United in July 1959 and after short spells at Hastings and Ramsgate, took a pub in Sussex before returning to Ireland to run the bar at Queen's University.

UTILITY PLAYERS

A utility player is one of those particularly gifted footballers who can play in several or even many different positions. Two of Portsmouth's earliest utility players were Jock Hunter and Thomas Bowman. Hunter joined Pompey from Preston North End and though primarily a half-back, turned out at both inside and centre-forward positions. Thomas Bowman, signed from Southampton was equally at home in any of the defensive positions.

During the club's Championship-winning seasons of 1948–49 and 1949–50, Reg Pickett wore seven different numbered shirts.

After the mid 1960s, players were encouraged to become more adaptable and to see their roles as less stereotyped. At the same time, however, much less attention came to be paid to the implication of wearing a certain numbered shirt and accordingly some of the more versatile players came to wear almost all the different numbered shirts at some stage or another, although this did not necessarily indicate a vast variety of positions.

In the modern game, Peter Denyer who played in 144 League and Cup games for Pompey between 1975 and 1978 wore every outfield shirt.

V

VENABLES, TERRY

Club chairman Terry Venables, who is also in charge of the Australian

national team, was a stylish player with four London clubs and won an FA Cup and League Cup winners' medal during his playing career.

He became the first player to represent England at five different levels – Schoolboy, Amateur, Youth, Under-23 and Full.

His two full caps came when he was a Chelsea player but in 1966 after 237 first team appearances for the Stamford Bridge club, he joined Tottenham Hotspur.

He won an FA Cup winners' medal the following year as they beat his former club Chelsea before joining Queen's Park Rangers in the summer of 1969. Five years later he ended his playing career with Crystal Palace and with whom he began his first managerial appointment.

He took the Eagles from the Third to the First Division before taking charge at Queen's Park Rangers. He led the Loftus Road club to the FA Cup Final and the Second Division title. In May 1984 he received a huge offer to manage Barcelona, where he won the Spanish League Championship in his first season and the following year took the club to the European Cup Final.

He returned to England to manage Spurs where his contribution was always full of incident and culminated in public conflict with Alan Sugar in 1993. His eventual dismissal provoked fierce protest among his many devoted fans but in 1994 he was appointed England's coach. He led the nation to the semi-finals of the European Championships before making way for Glenn Hoddle.

VICTORIES IN A SEASON: HIGHEST

In the 1961–62 season, Portsmouth won twenty-seven of their forty-six League fixtures to win the Third Division Championship, the highest in the club's history. They equalled this achievement in 1982–83 when they again won the Third Division title.

VICTORIES IN A SEASON: LOWEST

Pompey's poorest performance was in 1958–59 when they won only six matches out of their forty-two League games and finished bottom of the First Division.

W

WALSH, PAUL

A skilful ball playing forward, his natural talent was clear at an early age and after starting with Charlton Athletic, he won Under-21 and full England caps after a move to Luton Town.

He was the PFA's Young Player of the Year in 1984, the year of his big money move to Liverpool. Despite winning a European Cup winners' medal in 1985, a League Championship medal in 1986 and a League Cup

winners' medal in 1987, he was often left on the fringes and in February 1988, he joined Spurs for £500,000. He played in 155 first team games for the White Hart Lane club before joining Portsmouth as a £400,000 slice of Darren Anderton's transfer to Spurs in May 1992.

After playing an integral role in Pompey's spirited bid for promotion to the Premier League in 1992–93, a season in which he scored nine goals in forty-three games but made many more for Guy Whittingham, he joined Manchester City for £700,000 in March 1994.

It proved an inspired move as he linked well with Rosler and Beagrie but after playing in just three matches of the 1995–96 season, he was part of the deal which saw Gerry Creaney go to Maine Road and he return to Fratton Park for a second spell. He seemed to give the team more edge, but his season was cut short by a knee ligament injury.

WARNER, JACK

Full-back Jack Warner signed for Preston North End in 1902, from local side, St Michael's, and gradually gained a place in the club's League side during the 1903–04 season. However, midway through the following season, he found himself in the reserve side and so moved to Southampton. He acquitted himself well in the sixteeen games he played for the Saints, but the Southampton directors considered him suspect, due to a nagging knee injury and he moved to Portsmouth.

He made his debut for Pompey in a 4–0 Southern League victory over Plymouth on the opening day of the 1906–07 season. An ever-present during the 1911–12 season when the club finished runners-up in the Southern League Second Division, Warner proved the Saints' directors wrong, remaining at Pompey as a player until 1915. He made 300 appearances for the club scoring fifteen goals, later becoming their trainer.

WARTIME FOOTBALL

First World War

In spite of the outbreak of war in 1914, the major football leagues embarked upon their planned programme of matches for the ensuing season and these were completed on schedule at the end of April the following year. Pompey finished the 1914–15 season in seventh place in the Southern League.

The following season, the club played in the South West Combination, but teams often arrived late for matches and on occasions, short of players. In 1916–17, Pompey joined the London Combination and though they beat Watford 8–3 and Queen's Park Rangers 7–1, they suffered some heavy defeats, losing 10–0 to Tottenham Hotspur, 9–0 at Watford and 7–0 at Brentford. At the end of that season, the London clubs suddenly decided that they were no longer going to travel to Portsmouth or Southampton and so Pompey played the next two seasons in the South Hants War League.

Second World War

In contrast to the events of 1914, once war was declared on 3 September 1939, the Football League programme of 1939–40 was immediately suspended and the government forbade any major sporting events, so that for a while there was no football of nay description.

Pompey had begun the 1939–40 season with a 2–1 win over Blackburn Rovers and wore numbered shirts for the first time in a League match. They then lost their next two League games, 2–0 at Derby County and 2–1 at Bolton Wanderers. The FA later sanctioned two regional competitions but with travel often difficult and players guesting for clubs, the game became somewhat haphazard.

One player who 'guested' for Portsmouth was Andy Black of Hearts and Scotland and in a 16–1 win over Clapton Orient, he scored eight goals. In 1942, the club reached the War Cup Final but lost 2–1 to Brentford in front of a 72,000 crowd at Wembley. Seven-a-side matches developed during factory dinner breaks and with a number of Pompey players involved, money was raised for both the London Bomb Children and the Aid to China Fund.

The war years also saw the emergence of Jimmy Dickinson and the election of General Montgomery as Pompey's president. They had also taken their toll on the club's kit which needed replacing. Rationing was still in force and so the club appealed for 500 clothing coupons which eventually came in, allowing Portsmouth to resume League football in 1946.

WATSON, DAVE

Born in Bannockburn, inside-forward Dave Watson joined Portsmouth from Sunderland in 1920 and made his debut in a 1–0 defeat at Reading in January 1921. However, it was 1922–23 before he became a regular in the Pompey side.

The following season, when Portsmouth won the Third Division championship, Watson was one of three ever-presents, scoring twelve goals. Though not a prolific scorer, he scored sixty-three goals in 298 League and Cup outings, scoring his first hat-trick for the club on 6 October 1928 in a 3–2 win over Sheffield Wednesday.

Sharing a benefit with fellow Scot Jimmy Martin in September 1926, Watson played his last game for the Fratton Park club on 28 September 1929, when he scored Pompey's goal in a 4–1 home defeat by Everton.

WEBB, NEIL

Neil Webb's career had begun with Reading before he signed for Portsmouth for £87,500 in June 1982. Making his debut against Sheffield United on the opening day of the 1982–83 season, Webb scored one of the goals in a 4–1 win for Pompey. He went on to play in all but four of the games that season, as Pompey were crowned Third Division champions.

Scoring regularly from midfield, Webb topped the club's goalscoring charts in 1984–85 with sixteen goals, including four doubles, and another two in a 3–0 League Cup win over Wimbledon. At the end of that season, he joined Brian Clough's Nottingham Forest and, after winning eighteen caps, moved to Manchester United for £1.5 million.

After a few games at the beginning of the 1989–90 season, he damaged an Achilles tendon while playing for England and at one time, it looked like ending his career. However, he fought back to regain his place and was in the United side that won the FA Cup. Never quite the same player, he returned to Nottingham Forest in 1992 after a disagreement with Alex Ferguson.

WEDDLE, JACK

At a time when Portsmouth appeared destined to suffer relegation in their initial season as a First Division club, Jack Weddle, discovered while playing in north eastern junior football, was introduced as leader of the attack with such results that the fear of relegation was quickly banished. After scoring the only goal of the game on his debut against Burnley, seven consecutive matches were played without defeat. In all, Weddle scored nine goals in fourteen matches and proved the chief factor in preserving the club's senior status.

In 1929–30 he was an ever-present and the club's leading scorer with twenty-one League goals, including his first hat-trick for Pompey in the 7–1 win over Burnley on 4 January 1930. The following season he struck up a great understanding with Jimmy Easson and scored twenty-four goals, netting another hat-trick in a 4–3 win over Blackpool. In 1931–32 he headed the scoring charts again and netted all three goals in a 3–0 defeat of West Ham United.

He continued to top the club's scoring charts for the next four seasons, equalling his record of twenty-four goals in a season in 1934–35 when he scored hat-tricks against Preston North End (Home 4–0) and Huddersfield Town (Home 5–0).

Regarded as one of the best centre-forwards in the south, Jack Weddle was allowed to join Blackburn Rovers on a free transfer at the end of the 1937–38 season. He had made 368 League appearances for the club and scored a record 171 goals with another thirteen in twenty-eight Cup ties.

WESTERN LEAGUE

Portsmouth were Western League champions in 1900–01, 1901–02 and 1902–03, when the feat was marked by the presentation of a special banner.

WHITTINGHAM, GUY

He joined Portsmouth in June 1989, when he bought himself out of the Army for £450. He had previously played non-League football for Yeovil  and Waterlooville. He made his League debut in the goalless draw at home to Stoke City on 26 August 1989 when he came on as a substitute for Mark Kelly.

He top scored in his first season with 23 goals, including a hat-trick in a 3–3 draw at Oldham Athletic. He continued to be a prolific scorer and in 1992–93 when Pompey finished third in the new First Division of the Football League, he created a new club scoring record with 42 goals in 46 games. He scored all four goals in the 4–1 home win over Bristol Rovers and hat-tricks against Bristol City (Away 3–3) Luton Town (Away 4–1) and Peterborough United (Home 4–0).

He had scored 104 goals in 189 games for Pompey when he signed for Aston Villa for 1.2 million in the summer of 1993.

He had hardly established himself at Villa Park when he was loaned out to Wolverhampton Wanderers before joining Sheffield Wednesday for £700,000 in December 1994. A well-respected striker, he has now moved into midfield but is still continuing to score at a useful rate.

WILSON, ALEX

Scotsman Alex Wilson was signed from his home town team Buckie Rovers in November 1950. He made a disastrous start to his Pompey career, making his debut in a 5–0 defeat at West Bromwich Albion. Over the next few seasons, he only appeared in a handful of games before winning a regular place in 1956–57. However, he had obviously made an

124

impression before establishing himself in the Portsmouth side, because on 25 May 1954, he won his one and only Scottish cap in a 2–1 win over Finland in Helsinki.

Wilson played in 381 games for Pompey, making his last appearance in a goal-less draw at Derby County in April 1967. He left Fratton Park at the end of the season to play non-League football with Chelmsford City.

WORRALL, FRED

Probably one of the most superstitious players was Fred Worrall. He never went to an away match without three or four mascots and he took them out with him at Wembley in 1939 when Portsmouth beat Wolverhampton Wanderers 4–1. In fact, Worrall was the only survivor of Pompey's 1934 final side.

Warrington-born Worrall should have begun his first class career with Bolton Wanderers but owing to a technical flaw in his registration, the engagement was cancelled and he was signed on by Oldham Athletic. Having gained valuable experience with the Latics for three years, he was transferred to Portsmouth in September 1931 and made his debut in the home defeat by Everton a few days later. Quick off the mark and a good crosser of the ball, he scored a number of goals for Pompey, with his best season being 1934–35 when he netted fifteen in the League.

After appearing in the club's FA Cup final defeat of 1934, he played for England against Holland and the following season against Northern Ireland, scoring in both games which were won by England. He appeared in 341 games for Portsmouth, scoring seventy-four goals, before later playing for Crewe Alexandra.

WORST START

The club's worst ever start to a season was in 1937–38. It took sixteen League games to record the first victory of the season, drawing just five and losing ten of the opening fixtures. The dismal run ended with a 4–0 success over Derby County at Fratton Park on 20 November 1937 and though the club lost their next match 5–0 at Wolverhampton Wanderers, they were unbeaten in their next eight fixtures and ended the season in nineteenth place.

X

X

In football X traditionally stands for a draw. The club record for the number of draws in a season was in 1981–82 when they managed nineteen draws out of forty–six matches in a season which saw them finish thirteenth in the Third Division.

XMAS DAY

There was a time when football matches were regularly played on Christmas Day but in recent years, the game's authorities have dropped the fixture from their calendar.

The last time Portsmouth played on Christmas Day was 1957 when they lost 7–4 to Chelsea at Stamford Bridge in a game in which the Fratton Park club were 5–1 down at half-time.

Pompey's first five seasons in the Southern League saw them play Tottenham Hotspur on Christmas Day, and in 1908 William Reid scored a hat-trick in a 6–2 win over Southend. The club's heaviest defeat on Christmas Day came in 1922 when they lost 7–1 at Brighton.

Y

YOUNGEST PLAYER

The youngest player to appear in a first class fixture for Portsmouth is Clive Green, who played in the Third Division match against Wrexham (Away 0–2) on 21 August 1976 when he was sixteen years 259 days old.

Green is also the club's youngest League goal scorer. When sixteen years 280 days old, he netted Pompey's goal in a 1–1 draw at home to Lincoln City on 11 September 1976.

YOUTH CUP

Though Portsmouth have never reached the final of the FA Youth Cup they have won through to the semi-final stage of the competition on two occasions. The first came in 1961–62 when after beating Newcastle United 1–0 in the first leg at Fratton Park, they went down 4–2 in the return at St James' Park. The club's second appearance in the semi-final came in 1989–90 when they lost 4–1 on aggregate to Middlesbrough.

Z

ZENITH

Few fans will argue over which moment has been the finest in the club's history. For after winning the FA Cup in 1939, Pompey joined the select few clubs to have won the League Championship in successive years, winning the title in 1948–49 and 1949–50.

ZENITH DATA SYSTEMS CUP

The Zenith Data Systems Cup replaced the Simod Cup for the 1989–90 season. Pompey's first match saw them entertain Wimbledon but despite constant pressure from the home side, the Dons won 1–0. In 1990–91, Pompey visited Oxford United, the Manor Ground club winning 1–0 in a match played in front of only 1,055 spectators.

In 1991–92, Pompey travelled to Plymouth Argyle and went down 1–0 to their Second Division rivals. It was the club's last game in a competition which had seen them lose all three games and fail to score a single goal.